"DO NO HARM"

APPLIES TO NURSES TOO!

This book should be a MUST read for all senior level nursing students before graduation. By giving the graduates the proper tools to defuse the bullies and their behaviors, we may one day stop eating our young.

Kathryn Bommer MSN, BS, RN, PHRN, EMT-P, TNCC
Staff Nurse, Emergency Department

This book is a must read for nursing students, bedside nurses and nurse managers. Bulling has wrapped its insidious tentacles around nursing, the most noble of professions far too long. Finally someone has cared enough to acknowledge this villainous behavior and is insightful enough to devise a blue print for profoundly diminishing the presence and effects of bullying. Renee writes passionately while providing tools and strategies for the bullied and those in positions of authority to positively impact the environment in which nurses work. Well done and much needed!

Michael Coppola, MSN, RN

It is said over and over "nurses eat their young." I can't stand that and am working in my career to correct that lunacy. But the author really delves into the toxicity of that truism and how it spills over into patient care.

Amazon customer

Excellent book. *"Do No Harm" Applies to Nurses Too* focuses attention on a real, but mostly silent problem. Every patient, every leader in a hospital should be concerned. Renee Thompson explains why. Care delivery in hospitals has become extremely complex and teamwork is required for patient safety and best outcomes. Bullying not only damages the individual, but also damages the team. Weakening team members weakens the team and harms patients. Renee Thompson provides real life examples and practical tools for individuals and for organizations. I highly recommend this book.

Amazon customer

Dr. Thompson shines an illuminating light on the rarely discussed, dark world of nurse-to-nurse bullying. *"Do No Harm"* not only defines intimidation and maltreatment situations in both the work and school environments, but also offers practical, reality-based solutions to support the culture of nurturing and mutual respect that is vital to the nursing profession. Renee's passion for the wellness of the nursing profession is obvious as she courageously speaks out against workplace bullying using a light-hearted, amusing approach to encourage a supportive nurse-to-nurse atmosphere.

Rebecca B. Shaheen DNP, MSN, RN
Professor, CCAC Nursing
Owner, Relax in the Attic LLC Wellness Center

I love my nursing job, but the toxic workplace behavior that went unchecked for years drove me to consider resignation. I'm so glad I read Renee's book, which validated my experience and taught me useful skills. I applied Renee's practical, concrete advice to my situation. My workplace is beginning to change for the better, and I'm not leaving! Renee's guidance has been significant in helping make this happen.

Laura Y., RN

I thoroughly enjoyed Renee's seminar on bad behavior and communication as presented to CCBC faculty in professional development. I have read her book, *"Do No Harm" Applies to Nurses Too!* and incorporated many items in my communication lecture for practical nursing students.

Sally Fitzgerald, MSN, RN, CCM
Associate Professor, Nursing
Community College of Beaver County

The book, *"Do No Harm" Applies to Nurses Too!,* provides the reader with an amazing look at the ugly that exists in nursing— the ugly that every nurse knows but isn't always willing to admit. Not only does this book include amazing stories about nurse bullying but Renee shares practical strategies to help individuals and organization stop the cycle of nurse bullying!

Tina Durham, RN

"DO NO HARM"
APPLIES TO NURSES TOO!

STRATEGIES TO
PROTECT AND BULLY-PROOF
YOURSELF AT WORK

Renee Thompson, DNP, RN, CMSRN

This book was written and published in
partnership with inCredible Messages, LP
www.inCredibleMessages.com

To contact the author, Renee Thompson, visit
    Website...... : www.rtconnections.com
    LinkedIn ..... : Linkedin.com/in/rtconnections
    Facebook... : http://RTConnect.fbfollow.me
    Twitter .... : twitter.com/rtconnections
    Blog............ : blog.rtconnections.com

To contact the publisher, inCredible Messages Press, visit
www.inCredibleMessages.com

Printed in the United States of America

ISBN 978-0-9847983-5-3 Paperback
ISBN 978-0-9847983-6-0 e-Book

-Self Help   -Personal Growth

Book Coaching and Editing: Bonnie Budzowski, inCredible Messages, LP

Cover Design: Bobbie Fox, Bobbie Fox, Inc.

Interior Design: inCredible Messages, LP

To protect confidentiality, names and some details of the stories in this book have been changed.

DEDICATION

This book is for you and for all of the other nurses who struggle with the ugly in nursing: while we are kind to patients, we can be horrific to each other.

ACKNOWLEDGEMENTS

I wrote this book because you told me to—you and all of the other nurses who at some point in their careers have been treated badly by another nurse. As I listened to your horror stories of being "eaten alive" by your colleagues, a voice started to grow within me. I couldn't just sit back and say, "Well, that's just the way it is in nursing." I felt compelled to do something to help. I've spent half a lifetime lending an empathetic ear to nurses, and this book allows me to reach the many of you who perhaps don't have anyone to go to for help.

I've had a voice in my head for a long time and without the support of a small village, that voice would still be within me and not on these pages. Some colleagues have supported my efforts even when others suggested I shouldn't write about nursing's "dirty little secret." I owe a special debt of gratitude to Joanne Turka (my hero), Lynn George, Christine Deschamps, and Deb Wolf for their candid feedback and tireless support. Without their belief in me, I'd probably still be on page one. I also want to recognize the many nurses who shared their stories with me in the hope that they can play a part in helping the current and future generation of nurses—special air hug to you all.

If it weren't for Bonnie Budzowski of inCredible Messages, my own personal coach and cheerleader, this book would still be a voice in my head. Bonnie coached me through the book writing process from start to finish. She gently kept me on track, challenged my current way of thinking, and helped me improve my writing skills. (I still have trouble with fuzzy pronouns!) I owe her a great deal of gratitude for her commitment to helping me finish this book despite her own unexpected challenges.

There are friends and there are FRIENDS. Dina, Kim (still Kimmy to me), and I have known each other almost since birth. They are not nurses, although I've tried to convince them to join us. They love and accept me unconditionally—no matter what. When I've canceled an evening out because of work, they just had drinks without me—never judging and always supporting. Maybe it's because they believe in what I'm doing or maybe it's because they secretly hope that I will become rich and famous and have a beach house in Maui with a continuous open invitation to visit. Thanks for being my friends.

And finally, there are some people we meet due to circumstance and others we meet because it's our destiny. It was destiny that allowed me to meet my husband, Ashley. Without his selfless support, I would not be where or who I am today. He is the kindest human I know and truly inspires me to always choose the right path, always see the good in people, and always appreciate the little things.

They say the true validation that you've done a good job as a parent is to look at the success of your children. My definition of success is simple—if you are a good human, you are successful. That being said, I can say that I'm a good parent because I have two adult daughters, Kaitlin and Courtney, who humble me every day (well, almost) by their kindness, generosity, and empathy for others, especially strangers in need. They are a testament that young people do care, that they can be kind to other humans, and that they do want to make a difference.

And of course, the family I grew up with—my parents, sisters, and brothers. Although scattered across the country, they would drop everything if someone in the family needed them. Blood is blood!

My friends' and family's reminder of the goodness in people gave me the encouragement to write this book from my heart and to know that I was doing a good thing.

CONTENTS

CHAPTER 1

NURSES ARE EATING THEIR YOUNG—EVERYWHERE

Conducting focus groups with students and newly graduated working nurses across a large health system years ago, I got an earful about the realities that nursing students and new nurses face. The picture wasn't pretty. As a facilitator, nurse, and nurse educator, I had a hard time remaining objective while listening to stories of public criticism, lack of support, unrealistic workloads, exclusion, and pure rudeness. Some stories pointed to a disregard for patient safety as well as a disregard for common decency. It seemed every participant had a story to tell, each more horrific than the one before.

The experience created a conundrum for me. The purpose of the focus groups was to gather information for a graduate nurse residency program I was developing, not to explore or address bullying in a prestigious health system. Yet, how could I ignore a multitude of stories about behavior that was both deeply hurtful to new nurses and a safety risk to patients?

One particular account haunted me. It involved a nurse I'll call Cathy whom I knew by reputation. Cathy was an experienced nurse with excellent clinical skills. She worked on a busy surgical unit that saw its share of complex patients. Cathy was the nurse who was assigned the toughest cases. However, Cathy was also known as the bully on the unit. Word got around to both students and new graduates to stay away from Cathy. Heck, even the instructors didn't like to assign their students to Cathy's patients because Cathy was cruel.

Although I knew about Cathy's reputation, I was still appalled that three different focus groups comprised of students and new graduates identified Cathy as a queen bully. One student shared that Cathy had pulled her aside to say she hated student nurses and to stay out of her way. One student reported that when paired with Cathy, a different nurse on the unit whispered to her not to go to Cathy for anything but to come to her instead because Cathy "will just eat you up." Another participant shared that as a new nurse she had asked to be transferred to a different unit after one week due to Cathy's verbal outbursts at the nurses' station.

What should I do with this information? As you know, focus groups are intended to be confidential meetings for the purpose of gathering information, not for singling out individuals or solving problems. How could I fail to let somebody in a leadership position know about the impact Cathy's behavior was having on the nursing staff? Surely if I were in an authority position, I would want to know that three different groups of current and future nurses shared horror stories about Cathy.

I decided to discreetly contact a nursing director while protecting the identities of my focus group participants. By providing information about this situation, I would clearly make a positive impact on the nursing staff at this hospital as well as on prospective employees. I was also sure that the director would receive this information well and thank me for sharing.

I did receive thanks for coming forward, but the solution suggested by the director was unexpected, to say the least. The response was downright shocking.

The director suggested sending the entire nursing staff (all 65 of them) to a four-hour workshop on how to handle a bully! I was taken aback and didn't know how to respond. Stumbling over my words, I observed that perhaps the solution should be to address the issues with Cathy, not the 65 nurses working on the unit with her. I kept thinking, "Instead of helping the staff cope with the bully, just fire the bully!"

I could not fathom why someone would keep one nurse at the expense of 65. It defied logic, until I remembered we were in the midst of a severe nursing shortage. Not only was Cathy a skilled nurse, she worked a lot of overtime and could be counted on to carry a big load. Losing Cathy meant losing the equivalent of two nurses.

Several months later, I learned that although there was a discussion about Cathy among hospital leaders, nothing was done. Nobody went to training to learn how to deal with bullies, and nothing happened to Cathy. In fact, as I write, Cathy is still working on the same unit. Her bullying legacy continues.

Do you have a "Cathy" in your workplace? Have you been the target of a bully like Cathy? Even if you have not been the target, have you witnessed any of the following?

- Nurses screaming and yelling at other nurses
- Nurses calling others derogatory names
- Nurses gossiping
- One nurse rolling his or her eyes behind another's back
- A charge nurse assigning unequal work loads
- One nurse refusing to help another with information or patient care
- Some nurses "dumping" on others

- Some nurses excluding others from activities such as lunch breaks or social events

These are just a few unprofessional behaviors that may be considered acts of bullying. While some behaviors are obvious, others can be subtler. However, all are damaging.

If you've been the target of such behaviors, I don't have to tell you how hurtful they are. You know the blow these behaviors can inflict upon your self-confidence, your performance, and even your health.

I wonder, however, if you believe these behaviors are acceptable, that they are simply a reality in healthcare. Or do you believe, as I do, that bullying is unacceptable and must be stopped? If you believe bullying is intolerable and want to take action to protect yourself from attack, this book is for you.

Nurses bullying nurses, also known as horizontal violence, has a long history in our profession. All kinds of reasons (excuses) are given, including the idea that bullying is a rite of passage and/or that bullying toughens nurses up to survive in a challenging profession.

New nurses may think the bully problem lies with specific individuals or organizations and that changing jobs will solve their bullying problems. Research suggests the same bad behaviors are present anywhere you go. Bullying is pervasive in healthcare; it doesn't discriminate based on position, experience, or location; and it is often kept quiet in an organization. Nurse-to-nurse bullying has been accepted for a long time, but the problem is finally getting the attention it deserves. Nurses are starting to speak up and are trying to do something to eliminate bullying in the nursing profession.

Bullying in nursing is a complex problem, with deep roots in the culture of healthcare. Everyone involved has a responsibility to contribute to positively changing the culture. While your own efforts may not be enough to change an organization, you can make a real difference—especially when it comes to yourself and your work unit.

Throughout the pages of this book, you'll learn to recognize bullying behavior, encounter strategies to cope if you are the target, and gain tools to reduce bullying in your workplace environment.

Bullying comes in many different packages. This book will show you how to deal with the most common behaviors in ways that strengthen your moral courage while preserving your integrity, self-esteem, and professional practice.

> *We've got to dispel this myth that bullying is just a normal rite of passage.*
>
> ~ President Barack Obama

OFFICIAL GROUPS ARE TAKING ACTION

While this book will focus on what individual nurses and managers can do to address bullying, it might be encouraging to know you are not alone in recognizing that bullying must be stopped. Official groups in healthcare are beginning to set standards to increase professionalism and decrease bullying behavior.

For example, in 1983, The American Nurses Association instituted a code of ethics that governs the behavior and expectations for all nurses. This code of ethics is a roadmap, a compass that guides nurses in the right direction. When someone becomes a nurse, he or she is expected to behave in accordance with this set of professional standards. In a sense, these standards validate the profession and protect the people nurses serve.

Provision 1 of the code states:

> The nurse, in all professional relationships, practices with compassion and respect for the inherent dignity, worth and uniqueness of every individual, unrestricted by considerations of social or economic status, personal attributes, or the nature of health problems.

Provision 1 further details the expectations for relationships with colleagues and other members of the healthcare team. This provision tells us that compassion and respect go beyond patients—they extend to every person nurses interact with in their work environments. Words such as *integrity-preserving*, *harassment*, *caring relationships*, and *fair treatment* are embedded in the text and speak clearly about how nurses are expected to behave at work.

Hospitals should be safe havens for patients, not places where unprofessional behavior, such as intimidation, insulting, swearing, and yelling lead to mistakes. In 2008, The Joint Commission, a non-profit organization that accredits and certifies thousands of healthcare organizations, mandated that healthcare organizations develop codes of conduct that specifically address workplace bullying. Requirements include educating staff regarding professional behavior, holding individuals accountable for behavior, instituting "zero tolerance" for disruptive behavior, and documenting attempts to address bullying.

In 2009, The Joint Commission added leadership standards to further address and mitigate workplace bullying. In addition to codes of conduct, leaders must adopt a process for managing bullying behaviors.

In 2001, the American Association of Critical-Care Nurses (AACN) made a commitment to establish healthy work environments in acute care organizations. Initially, their commitment was made to address the worsening nursing shortage due to nurses leaving the profession in part because of hostile work environments.

The AACN's publication provides a roadmap for clinical practice and professional behavior. The report, drawing from published and unpublished data, demonstrates that nearly three out of four errors in hospitals can be linked to human factors associated with interpersonal interactions. The recommendations address the severity of disruptive, disrespectful behavior within healthcare organizations and encourage a commitment to collaborative, respectful practice. The AACN ends the report with a call to action, asking nurses to, "develop relationships in which individuals hold themselves and others accountable to professional behavioral standards."

While bullying has been present in healthcare for many years, the recent actions of these official groups may indicate that it's getting worse. Certainly more and more laypeople are becoming aware of the bullying that takes place in healthcare. One nurse told me a patient asked her how bad the bullying was in that hospital. He had heard, "Nurses eat their young." The patient asked the nurse if this was really true. How was the nurse to respond? Should she lie and deny that claim or tell the truth and have the patient worry about the care he was going to receive in a hospital where nurses were mean to each other?

IT'S TIME FOR THE BULLYING TO STOP

What would Florence Nightingale say if she saw how horribly nurses treat each other? Would she say, "Well that's just the way it has always been?" Perhaps she would say that we need to do something about the way nurses treat each other and that our duty, our ethical responsibility, is to eradicate bad behavior as Nightingale eradicated death from poor hygiene (well, almost).

Bullying leaves nasty fingerprints on individuals, healthcare organizations, the nursing profession, and patients. Its mark is damaging and long lasting.

> *Criticism and pessimism destroy families, undermine institutions of all kinds, defeat nearly everyone, and spread a shroud of gloom over entire nations.*
>   ~ Gordon B. Hinckley

BULLYING DAMAGES INDIVIDUALS

Individuals who are victims of bullying can suffer emotional distress such as depression, anxiety, feelings of helplessness, and despair. Emotional distress often leads to physical distress, including headaches, gastric upset (diarrhea, vomiting), and insomnia. Even neck and back pain can be linked to emotional distress caused by workplace bullying. Victims may cope by changing organizations, engaging in non-healthy behaviors (overeating, drinking, smoking), or quitting nursing all together.

Kaitlin, a new nurse, approached me after a presentation on horizontal violence. She had just finished orientation. Kaitlin was scheduled the next day for her first night shift without her preceptor. The look on Kaitlin's face told me she was petrified. I could see she was having trouble articulating without crying, so I pulled her into an empty classroom.

As Kaitlin was telling me about the hazing on her unit, she sobbed. She didn't know what to do because the night staff did most of the hazing. Kaitlin's preceptor had been able to protect her in the past, but now that she was off orientation, Kaitlin would be forced to defend herself alone. One of the unit nurses had warned her not to even ask any of them for help—that she was on her own.

Although she asked for my advice, Kaitlin told me that she had already made the decision to call off for the entire weekend. She had been experiencing diarrhea for days as she anticipated her first shifts off orientation. She felt weak, worried, and run-down before she even officially began her new assignment. Kaitlin felt she didn't have the ability to focus on taking care of her patients, knowing she had to work with the bully nurses.

BULLYING DAMAGES ORGANIZATIONS

Leaders of one healthcare organization once bragged about their awesome recruitment strategies and high hire rates. They had the best marketing, best billboards, best recruitment events, and best commercials in the area. The organization hired over 800 nurses several years in a row across their system. Sounds great, right? Then somebody finally asked the question, "If we are doing such a great job getting nurses in the door, why are we still so short staffed?" One answer? Resignation rates were higher than hire rates. The organization could get them in, but they couldn't keep them. Bullying, which contributed to the turnover, is a costly organizational problem.

Some nurses who begin their jobs in environments plagued with bullies choose to suffer in silence for fear of retaliation. Others confront the issue. Many more quit. This creates the hamster wheel effect, where organizations lose nurses as fast as they get them in.

Conservative calculations estimate an organization must invest $60,000 to $80,000 for every nurse hired to get that nurse up-to-speed. In addition, nurses who fall victim to bullying but stay on the job have higher absenteeism. Replacing absentee employees creates additional costs for organizations, especially if the missing employees are in direct patient care.

Bullying Damages the Nursing Profession

Bullying behavior not only is a direct violation of a nurse's code of ethics, but the mere existence of it tarnishes the reputation of the nursing profession. Bullying has a negative effect on the recruitment of new nurses while it puts current nurses, good nurses, at risk for leaving the profession, putting the entire profession of nursing in jeopardy.

For example, Kim had dreamed of being a nurse ever since she was in grade school. Her mother and grandmother were retired nurses who used to share their stories about how wonderful it was to be a nurse helping patients, caring for others in times of need, assisting doctors, etc. When Kim was in high school, she started volunteering at a local hospital. She was so excited! However, it wasn't long before she witnessed the nursing staff members' bad behaviors. She started asking around and learned about the ugly in nursing. Kim learned about horizontal violence and the fact that it was widespread. Kim was devastated and gave up her dream of becoming a nurse.

Bullying Threatens Patient Safety

Ultimately, bad behavior is most damaging to patients. The Joint Commission identified that healthcare organizations with high rates of bullying behavior have worse patient outcomes due to increased medical errors. How? If you are the victim of bullying, you are not as likely to question a decision, ask for help, or learn from your colleagues.

According to the Institute of Medicine, approximately 200,000 patients die each year due to medical error. Estimates suggest that 80% of medical errors are due to communication. Bullying creates an environment where poor communication is the norm.

In the airline industry, a jumbo jet airplane would have to crash, killing all of its passengers, every Monday, Wednesday, and Friday to accumulate 200,000 deaths per year. Do you think the government would get involved in the airline industry if that happened? Perhaps that's why the government has become involved in the healthcare industry.

> *Courage is the most important of all the virtues, because without courage you can't practice any other virtue consistently. You can practice any virtue erratically, but nothing consistently without courage.*
> ~ Maya Angelou

THE SOLUTION BEGINS WITH MORAL COURAGE

If you're the target of a bully, I don't have to remind you that bullying is a serious problem with serious consequences. The issue has been kept under the covers for so long because nobody really knows how to deal with it. We know bullying is rampant, but bringing it into the open involves addressing personalities—not performance. It also involves feelings and emotions. It's much easier to tell a nurse he or she compromised sterile technique than it is to tell the same person that his or her language and tone is abrasive and disruptive.

Whether you are a target, a witness, and/or a manager, the bullying won't end until you and your colleagues find moral courage within yourselves and develop it. You must find the courage to take action for moral reasons, despite the risk of adverse consequences. Whatever your role in healthcare, you must develop the capacity to overcome fear and stand up for your core values and ethical obligations. You must be willing to address a problem that others ignore. As long as bullying is allowed to continue in silence, it will continue to grow as a problem.

Moral courage is so critical to addressing the bully problem that you'll see this symbol through-out the book as a reminder to tap into your moral courage.

I'm not claiming any of this will be easy. My commitment is to show you how, one step at a time. If you are feeling vul-nerable, don't worry: you don't have to eat the whole elephant at the outset. As you learn strategies and take one healthy step at a time, your moral courage will grow. For example, you'll learn how to display a sense of strength and self-confidence, even when you feel frightened and insecure. This alone will reduce the likelihood that a bully will find you an appealing target. You'll also learn to identify specific bullying behaviors and to strategize against those behaviors rather than against the people who act out the behaviors.

Bullying can be stopped!

This book offers a solution to begin the journey back to professional practice, caring for the sick, AND treating each other with the respect we all deserve.

> *Imagine a world where bullying doesn't exist. Where nurses go out of their way to support each other. Where everyone works well together. No. You're not dreaming. It is real—or at least can be.*

WHAT TO EXPECT FROM THIS BOOK

In this chapter, we've identified bullying behaviors and the damage they inflict on individuals, organizations, our profession, and our patients. We've seen that bullying is a pervasive problem in nursing that must be stopped. Whether you are a target, a manager, or a witness, you CAN make a difference. The rest of this book is devoted to showing you how.

In Chapter 2, we'll discuss how the term horizontal violence became a "nursing term." We'll also identify the two overarching horizontal violent behaviors: covert and overt. We'll break these behaviors into observable human actions you can recognize. Once you know the behaviors, you can begin to recognize, plan, and strategize your intervention.

In Chapter 3, we'll look at how bullies choose their targets. You'll learn what characteristics and behaviors bullies look for in a target. You'll lay the foundation you need to protect and "bully-proof" yourself.

In Chapter 4, we'll identify bully-proofing strategies to decrease your chances of becoming a target. You'll learn how to make yourself unattractive to a bully.

In Chapter 5, we'll discover why people bully, especially in the nursing profession. Learning to identify underlying characteristics of most bullies will help you protect yourself from the bully.

In Chapter 6, we'll profile the leading bullies in the nursing profession, along with their motives. In this chapter, you may recognize some of your co-workers!

In Chapter 7, we'll identify step-by-step strategies for coping with and eliminating bad behaviors. We'll take a closer look at overt and covert behaviors and explore strategies to address each.

In Chapter 8, we'll discuss what to do when you've tried everything, yet the bullying continues. At what point do you say enough is enough? We'll also take a closer look at the role of the unit manager and what he or she can do to decrease horizontal violence in the workplace.

In Chapter 9, we'll discuss what to do if you recognize bullying behavior in yourself. It can be difficult to accept that you might be contributing to some of the bullying on your unit. Good people sometimes find themselves bullying others for a variety of reasons.

In Chapter 10, we'll summarize the key steps to recognizing, coping with, and eliminating bullying behavior in the workplace. This chapter will leave you with actionable steps to immediately decrease your stress and anxiety, starting yourself down the path towards a healthier, happier work experience.

Follow this journey to a better place for you, your organization, the nursing profession, and the patients we all serve. This book will provide the strategies you need to stand up to bullying. It's up to YOU to provide the moral courage. This doesn't mean you have to publicly confront the biggest bully or put yourself in danger. Moral courage grows with small steps taken one at a time. Let's begin the journey together.

> *A journey of a thousand miles begins with a single step.*
> ~ Lao-tzu

CHAPTER 2

MEET THE BULLY FAMILY

Ask a group of nurses if they've heard of the term *horizontal violence*, and many will say, "No." Ask these same nurses if they've heard the phrase, "Nurses eat their young," and they will immediately nod their heads and begin talking.

Just Google the words *horizontal violence, vertical violence,* or *bullying,* and you will get a plethora of articles, blogs, and documents all linking nursing to this term. We know it's a big deal, but where did the term originate?

The term *horizontal violence* was coined by theorist Paolo Freire, author of *Pedagogy of the Oppressed,* an expert on oppression. While in Africa, Freire witnessed oppression of people not by the government, but by themselves. Rather than being oppressed in a top-down way, Freire witnessed people oppressing each other—peers oppressing peers. Freire's work takes an in-depth look at the dynamics between the oppressor and the oppressed.

Sandra Roberts, who has a Ph.D. in nursing, was the first to apply the term *horizontal violence* to nursing. She looked at how nurses treat each other and discovered similarities with the oppressed people in Africa, thereby labeling nurses with the villainous term.

Other nurses, seeking to understand bullying behavior in nursing, have conducted further research. Cheryl Dellasega, a Ph.D. prepared nurse practitioner, is well known for her work with relational aggression in females. Her book, *Mean Girls Grow Up*, explores how toxic behaviors begin in girlhood and continue into adulthood—and our profession. According to Dellasega, one reason bullying is pervasive in nursing is that nursing is primarily a female-dominated profession.

Whether you find yourself in a country in Africa or on a busy medical surgical nursing unit in the United States, the result of horizontal violence is the same: low self-esteem, diminished self-respect, emotional and physical pain. Nurse-to-nurse violence is destructive and must be stopped. We can no longer accept bad behaviors, become complacent with them, or even condone them by saying, "Well, that's the way it is around here," or "That's just the way she is. Ignore her." As nurses, witnesses, and managers, we must learn to recognize and name horizontal violence when we see it. Where to begin?

The First Step Against Bullying: Assess

The steps to a world where bullying doesn't exist are similar to the steps followed in the nursing process: you must assess before you plan, and you must plan before you intervene. You would never think of giving an anti-hypertensive without checking a blood pressure or giving Digoxin without checking a Digoxin level. Likewise, before we can begin to eliminate bullying in nursing, we must begin with an assessment.

Read through the list of behaviors on the following page. Place an "X" next to any behavior you have either experienced or witnessed happening to other nurses in your current work environment.

Assess Your Experience with Bullying

	Have you experienced or witnessed these behaviors?	
1	Being yelled at, criticized, or cursed at in front of others	
2	Being mocked or having a nurse roll his or her eyes at you or another nurse	
3	Receiving an uneven workload assignment, seemingly based on favoritism or harassment	
4	Having a nurse break your confidence by sharing private and/or embarrassing information	
5	Having a nurse withhold information from you or another nurse, causing a negative effect on performance	
6	Being excluded by certain nurses from routine lunches, celebratory or social events	
7	Having yours or others' accomplishments (such as awards or advanced degree completions) downplayed	
8	Being interrupted by specific nurses when talking	
9	Having your opinion or input ignored by certain nurses	
10	Seeing nurses treated nicely to their faces but mocked or insulted behind their backs	
11	Hearing nurses name calling, making ethnic slurs, jokes, or inappropriate sexual comments	
12	Getting teased or repeatedly reminded of your mistakes	
13	Being the target of gossip or rumors	
14	Receiving threats of physical violence	
15	Having nurses refuse to help you or other nurses with information or patient care	

Enter the total number of behaviors you've experienced or witnessed here: _____

The higher the total number, the more significant the bullying problem.

Please note that although we may experience and witness the above behaviors by physicians and other disciplines within healthcare, the focus of this book is on nurse-to-nurse bullying behaviors.

Meet the Bully Family: Overt and Her Ugly Stepsister Covert

As you can see from the assessment, bullying involves tangible behaviors, specific acts that are repeated by the same or different people. Bullying and all of its complexities boil down to observable human actions that can be categorized into behaviors. Once you know the categories/behaviors, you can recognize, plan, and strategize your intervention.

Behaviors are either overt or covert. Overt behaviors are easier to observe, whereas covert behaviors are more subtle. Any behavior that can be observed is considered overt. Yelling, making inappropriate comments, and issuing threats are examples of overt behaviors; we can see them and name them. In contrast, behaviors that are not readily observable are covert. Withholding information and excluding someone from a guest list are examples of covert behaviors.

Scientists dealing in Ethology (the study of animal behavior) categorize behaviors into three classifications: innate, learned, and complex.

Innate behaviors are genetically programmed and not likely to change. Salmon swimming upstream to lay their eggs, hatched sea turtles automatically moving towards the ocean at night, and dogs burying everything they get are examples of innate behaviors. This type of behavior is not impacted by experience. It is, in a sense, instinctual or automatic. Innate behavior is present in humans too. For example, stroke a newborn's cheek and the baby will move toward the touch in an attempt to find the mother's nipple.

Any behavior at the time of birth is considered innate; however, as the animal or individual grows, it learns other behaviors that allow it to adapt to certain situations. Learned behavior refers to a change in behavior that results over time and experience. For example, newborns cry instinctually when they are hungry or in pain. However, as newborns grow, they also learn to associate crying with comfort. Babies learn that if they cry, they get what they want both physically and emotionally. Both innate and learned behaviors are overt, or easily observable.

A third type of behavior, complex, separates humans from animals. Complex behaviors are more subtle and covert than overt behaviors. Covert behaviors are more difficult for others to observe.

While a baby's behavior is always overt, a teenager's is not! For example, when a teenager responds to a parent's advice by rolling his or her eyes behind the parent's back, the teenager is engaging in covert behavior. When it comes to bullying, covert behavior may seem milder but can actually prove to be a more detrimental way of bullying because, typically, the victim doesn't see it coming. In contrast to overt behavior in which anyone nearby can observe the action, in covert behavior only the person on the receiving end can readily witness the behavior.

The following example illustrates the difference between overt and covert behavior:

- OVERT BEHAVIOR
  I walk up to a man and slap him.

- COVERT BEHAVIOR
  I tickle the man's nose with a feather while he is sleeping, and he slaps himself.

Overt (active)	Covert (passive)
Yelling	Excluding others
Criticizing	Withholding information
Humiliating others	Assigning unfair workloads
Intimidating others	Refusing to help
Threatening others	Taking credit for somebody else's work
Bickering	Sabotaging
Blaming	Undermining
Openly raising eyebrows or rolling eyes	Using sarcasm
Gossiping	Downplaying accomplishments

Take a moment to return to the assessment you completed earlier on page 17. Spend some time considering each behavior and why it is considered overt or covert. Do you have more experiences in overt or covert bullying behaviors? By categorizing the behaviors you've either experienced or witnessed, you can start formulating strategies that will address the behavior category, thereby addressing the specific behavior. Over time, you will be able to quickly recognize behaviors as overt or covert, which will enable you to respond appropriately.

IDENTIFY OVERT BULLIES IN ACTION

Overt behavior in nursing involves openly antagonistic displays of aggressive verbal language or action in an inappropriate setting. Another way of understanding overt behavior is that if the behavior is experienced by more than one person, each person will be able to describe the behavior in a similar way. Examples of overt behaviors include yelling at somebody in the nurses' station, criticizing in front of a patient or colleague, making inappropriate jokes, and making sexual remarks or gestures.

I once witnessed a nurse in an executive leadership position throw a full-fledged temper tantrum. She literally jumped up and down while screaming at a group of nurses. My colleagues and I were dumbfounded and didn't know how to respond. We just stood there in disbelief that somebody in a leadership position would act in such a way. Trust me, those of us who were subjected to the temper tantrum all described it in similar ways later during lunch!

Note: Keep in mind that physical violence is overt behavior and can be the result of an escalated verbal assault. If you find yourself in a situation where you are physically unsafe, get out and find help. This is not the time to try to interpret the behavior type. Always think safety first. For our purposes, we will recognize physical violence as an overt behavior but will concentrate on the non-physical types.

When Lisa was a new nurse, she worked a steady 3 p.m. to 11 p.m. shift. Lisa was warned very early into her orientation about the night shift nurses. They were well known for hazing the new nurses, and Lisa was warned to be on guard. It was difficult enough for Lisa to learn how to be a real nurse, let alone be "on guard" against her colleagues. She thought that maybe the nurses were exaggerating a bit. Then Lisa had an experience with Norma that she'll never forget.

Norma was what you would call a well-seasoned nurse. She worked steady 11 p.m. to 7 a.m. and was almost always in charge. Rarely did you see Norma smile or offer to help anyone, especially a new nurse. It was as though she took pride in her stoic posture and stern appearance.

Lisa tried to avoid Norma completely and, for the first month, she did. Then, one night Norma approached her. "I see that I'm not in charge tomorrow night and that I'll be following you." Then she leaned in closer to Lisa, and with a smirk on her face, said, "You had better make sure you give me a good report or the rest of your time here will be a nightmare. Just wanted to warn you." Norma then gave Lisa a half smile and walked away.

Lisa had trouble sleeping that night, had diarrhea the next day, and couldn't eat a thing. Lisa almost called off. Even though she was still on orientation and was working with a preceptor, the preceptor was also intimidated by Norma and offered no additional support. Lisa was on her own to deal with Norma.

When Lisa got to work, she spent her entire shift making sure she knew everything about her patients: Lisa knew their histories, memorized their labs, read their consults, looked up each medication history, and even went through her patients' previous charts. Although Lisa did what she had to do for her patients, her mind was fixated on preparing for Norma.

As the end of her shift drew closer, Lisa's panic worsened. And then Lisa saw her. Norma walked right up to her and said, "Well, are you going to give me a good report or should I just read the charts myself?"

Lisa's mouth was so dry that she almost couldn't speak. Lisa meekly replied, "No, I'll give you a good report."

Lisa did give Norma a good report because she had spent her entire shift preparing to do so. When she finished answering Norma's gazillion questions, all Norma said was, "Not bad," and walked away. For Norma, this was a compliment, but it came at a great cost to Lisa.

It's a shame Norma didn't use her knowledge to teach others, mentor them, and support them through the learning process. Rather, she used her knowledge to intimidate students, new nurses, and even new medical interns. Norma's overt behavior of intimidation was tolerated on the unit and so it continued. Sadly, there are a lot of Normas out there.

Lisa worked in an acute care setting, but bullying is not isolated to any one healthcare setting. You will find the same bullying behaviors in homecare and managed care industries. In my own career, I found that no matter what position I held or what work I did, bullying nurses were everywhere.

At one point, I took a new job as a unit director in an acute care hospital. I didn't find out until two months into my new role that my unit had the worst overall reputation in the entire hospital. Poor performance, bad behavior, poor patient satisfaction, high turnover, and low retention plagued the unit. It was my job to turn it around.

One night I received a page from Rachel, one of my nurses, telling me that Christine, one of the other nurses, had just threatened her. Rachel was scared.

I knew there had been conflicts between Rachel and Christine in the past. They just didn't get along. On this particular night, however, things escalated. Christine, in the middle of the hallway, in front of patients and other staff members, said to

Rachel, "I know what shuttle you take and my boyfriend is going to meet you when you get off and beat the s*** out of you!" Not only did Christine make this threat, but she repeated it several times in front of witnesses.

Upon receiving Rachel's call, I contacted security who then escorted Rachel to her car. I was able to terminate Christine based on the threat to physical harm in front of multiple witnesses, two of whom were patients. When I brought Christine into my office to terminate her, however, she was shocked. Christine said she couldn't believe she could be fired just for "pretending" to threaten somebody. She was teasing Rachel and didn't know what the big deal was. "Can't she take a joke?"

Either Christine didn't see her behavior as heinous or she was backpedaling and trying to get out of a termination. In either case, Christine threatened another human being. The behavior was overt bullying, easily identified and witnessed by others. Unfortunately, many bullying incidents are not so easily recognized or eliminated.

Identify Covert Bullies in Action

Susan started her first job as a nurse with a large group of other new nurses who all graduated from the same associate program. At first, the group got together for happy hours, tried to get breaks at the same time, and even started a birthday club, celebrating once a month with a cake. After six months, Susan told everyone she was going back to school to get her Bachelor's Degree of Science in Nursing (BSN) and then continue on for her master's degree.

Susan definitely did not expect the response she received from her peers. Susan was excited and thought her colleagues would be too, but members of the group immediately tried to talk Susan out of her plans. Some of the nurses told Susan additional degrees were a waste of her time and money and that even as new associate degree nurses, they were better than some of the BSN nurses. A few nurses said something akin to, "Pretty soon we won't be good enough for you." Susan was disappointed in the reaction but didn't let this stop her from enrolling.

Soon after, Susan began to notice that when she went to the cafeteria for the group's usual break time, nobody was there. When she asked her peers about this, they said, "Oh. We met earlier. I guess we forgot to tell you." Then when a few happy hours were planned, the nurses again "forgot" to tell Susan. The pattern became clear when Susan's birthday month came and she never got a cake. Susan was being systematically excluded from social activities. Soon Susan stopped trying to be part of the group.

Bullies who use exclusion, as in Susan's case, aren't honest about their reasons for excluding someone. They use sarcasm, tell white lies (oh, we forgot to invite you), and try to avoid actual conflict with the person they are bullying.

What if . . .

One of the group of associate nurses had stuck up for Susan and encouraged the others to be happy for her instead of excluding and criticizing her? How might this action against bullying have impacted the outcome?

Once, when I was working as a nurse educator in a large hospital, I was the target of a particularly dangerous act of covert bullying. At the time, my role involved supporting all things neurological and diabetic, new hire development, and the education requirements for several nursing units. Occasionally when the census was high and staffing was low, I would be asked to staff one of the units as a bedside nurse. On one of those occasions, I was assigned to the neurological floor.

Although I had a good relationship with the staff nurses, I felt a few who were nice to my face were probably talking about me behind my back. I was the one responsible for their yearly competencies, ongoing education, and maintaining high standards of nursing care. In the eyes of a few staff nurses, my presence typically equaled more work. One of the nurses apparently thought she could get back at me with covert bullying.

I got report on my six patients from one of the nurses I suspected was talking behind my back. I asked a few questions about each patient, said goodbye and started my assessments.

When I tried to encourage my first patient to get up (as good practice to prevent debilitation, pneumonia, and blood clots), the patient said she didn't think she was allowed up. I checked her orders, which had her out of bed to a chair as tolerated.

I went back into the patient's room and encouraged her again. The patient said she would prefer not to get out of bed, especially since "they took out that tube." Not knowing what she was talking about, I went back through my report sheet, thinking that I must have missed something, but there was nothing mentioned about a "tube" being removed.

Knowing this patient had a recent hospital stay for hydrocephalus (fluid on the brain), I decided to check her back for any evidence of a previous lumbar drain. To my surprise, she had a small fresh bandage on her lower back. I learned that the patient indeed did have a lumbar drain that had been removed a few hours before my shift started. Getting this patient out of bed could have compromised her recovery.

In report, the nurse never told me that vital piece of information. I found out later that she deliberately withheld the information from me and was overheard saying, "She thinks she's so smart. Let's see if she can figure out she had a lumbar drain." Wow, a nurse deliberately didn't tell me about the lumbar drain to see if I could find it myself! She was testing my assessment skills and putting the patient in jeopardy at the same time. When I confronted the nurse about her omission, she denied it, saying that she did tell me, and that I must not have been paying attention.

What if . . .

Instead of trying to trick me, this nurse accepted that professional behavior takes precedence over personal likes and dislikes? How would things have been different if this nurse had made patient safety and care her top priority?

Please note: A blend of behaviors can be identified as both overt and covert. Imagine, for example, Judy, a new nurse, is giving her opinion to Sally, an experienced nurse, on how they can improve their hand washing rates, based on something she learned in school. Sally appears to be listening attentively to Judy. As soon as Judy turns away, however, Sally rolls her eyes at another colleague and mocks Judy. The eye rolling is an overt (observable) behavior but since Judy did not witness this act, it is a covert act. The problem here is that Judy thinks that her opinion is valued but may find out later that Sally is making fun of her, talking behind her back, and possibly undermining her value.

Action Step

Make a list of three of your experiences that you now think might be examples of bullying behavior. Then identify each as either overt or covert behavior. If you have difficulty deciding, ask yourself if you and a colleague shared the same experience, would you both describe it the same way. If so, the behavior is probably overt. If not, it is probably covert.

Behavior 1: _____

_____

Circle one: Overt   Covert

Behavior 2: _____

_____

Circle one: Overt   Covert

Behavior 3: _____

_____

Circle one: Overt   Covert

If you are like most nurses, you don't have trouble recalling incidents in which you have experienced or witnessed bully behavior. By categorizing each story as an example of overt or covert behavior, however, you are taking an initial step toward adopting specific strategies that can address the behavior itself, not the person.

In Chapter 3, you'll learn what characteristics and behaviors bullies look for in a target. You'll begin to lay the foundation you need to protect and "bully-proof" yourself.

BULLYING ATTRACTION FACTORS—WHO MAKES A GOOD TARGET?

> *Never be bullied into silence. Never allow yourself to be made a victim. Accept no one's definition of your life, but define yourself.*
>
> ~ Harvey S. Firestone

STOP!

As you begin this chapter, be clear about one thing: if you are a victim of a bully, it's NOT your fault! Make no mistake about it. The fault lies with the bully, not you. As you read the profiles of the targets who are attractive to bullies, you may recognize some of the characteristics or behaviors in yourself. You may even feel a sense of self-blame. If you do, please remember that we all may exhibit these behaviors from time to time, and they do not justify the destructive behaviors of the bully.

A preferred target of any bully, in healthcare or elementary school, has similarities to a preferred target in other crimes. The crime-victim dance involves an interplay of factors: behavior, opportunity, timing, and sometimes just bad luck. It is not appropriate to blame the victim. However, in most cases a potential victim can adopt behaviors that reduce his or her risk of being a target.

For example, a woman who walks hunched over at night, on a deserted street, in a bad neighborhood does not deserve to be mugged or raped. Her body posture, however, may signal to a perpetrator that this woman is vulnerable as a target. On the other hand, the woman may make behavioral choices that lessen her chances of being perceived as an attractive target, even in the bad neighborhood. Walking "tall" with shoulders back, holding her head high, and making eye contact with others are behaviors any person can undertake to decrease the chances of becoming a target in any neighborhood. The same is true on any healthcare unit.

The goal of this chapter is to identify how bullies pick their targets and then to identify strategies to help you minimize your chances of being picked. The strategies you will learn are similar to those police officers teach to reduce your chances of becoming the victim of a crime.

> *Cruelty, like every other vice, requires no motive outside of itself; it only requires opportunity.*
> ~ George Eliot

Profile of an Attractive Target

Police officers refer to many crimes as "crimes of opportunity." If a burglar wants to rob a house, for example, he or she may go from house to house, checking to see if any doors or windows are unlocked. When the burglar finds an open window or door, the house owners become victims of opportunity.

Criminals look for the easy target and then act. Some crimes of opportunity are more subtle than others. Let's say you happen to leave your purse open in the locker room. Somebody walks by, looks in, and takes your wallet. The perpetrator may not have been planning to commit a crime but responded to an opportunity.

In the same way, workplace bullies are perpetrators of crimes against targets, even if some bullying behaviors are not illegal. Some bullies seek victims consciously and methodically while others respond to opportunities they happen to stumble upon. And, as we shall see, some bullies "fall into" bullying behavior in an attempt to fit in and be accepted by their peers.

How do nurse bullies pick their targets? Are there similarities among targets that can be identified, understood, and behaviorally changed to protect and reduce the likelihood of becoming a target of bullying? Throughout the literature, a wide range of characteristics have been identified as attracting the attention of bullies. These include shyness, introversion, youth, old age, confidence, lacking confidence, minority status, and more.

A list of characteristics, however, is minimally helpful. It makes no sense to try to change characteristics that make you who you are. If you are an introvert or a minority, it's pointless to try to change these traits. However, you can change specific *behaviors* that you display in how you carry yourself and how you present yourself in certain environments.

For example, it is quite possible for an introvert to participate effectively in a conversation with strangers at a party, even if the introvert still prefers an evening with one or two good friends. The introvert can display skillful conversation *behavior* without changing temperament or personality.

If we turn from characteristics to behaviors that increase a person's chances of becoming a target of bullying, three typical behaviors stand out. Bullies are most often attracted to people who demonstrate the following behaviors:

- Displaying diminished self-confidence

- Demonstrating passive behavior

- Walking a different path

BULLY ATTRACTOR: DISPLAYING DIMINISHED SELF-CONFIDENCE

My husband, Ashley Thompson, a city police officer, offers programs on personal safety to help people decrease their chances of becoming victims of crime. His recommendations are based on a deliberate display of behaviors involving self-confidence.

Criminals are attracted to specific behaviors they interpret as diminished self-confidence. A criminal observes the behaviors of potential victims and looks for the one person who does not look confident. Whether that person is internally confident or not is moot. It's really about how that person appears. Slumping shoulders, eyes looking down, and overt displays of nervousness can give the appearance that a person lacks self-confidence. In a criminal's mind, a person not displaying confidence is weak, and therefore an easy target, an opportunity.

The same process takes place in nursing. A bully surveys a new group of nurses (in this case, new does not necessarily equal young or inexperienced). Bullies watch and wait, looking for the behaviors that indicate vulnerability. A person who displays diminished self-confidence can shine like a neon sign, alerting the bully to a likely next target.

For example, after working as a new nurse for almost a year, Diane was feeling more confident in her skills. Whenever Carol was around, however, Diane's confidence quickly wavered. Carol just had a way of making Diane feel stupid. Carol was quick to criticize her in front of other nurses and physicians; gave Diane a hard time when she gave report; and when she was in charge, Carol consistently gave Diane the worst assignment.

One day Diane was feeling particularly overwhelmed. In front of a physician Diane truly respected, Carol verbally attacked her because she didn't put a document in the fax machine the right way. Diane felt shocked that Carol had berated her for such a simple mistake and embarrassed because a respected physician was standing right there. Diane didn't want the physician to think she was stupid.

The physician saw that Diane was barely able to hold back the tears and called her over. She whispered something that Diane will never forget. The doctor asked Diane why she would let anyone who was obviously less intelligent, less respectful, and less professional than her bring her to tears.

The doctor then said, "Hold your head up high and never again allow anyone to make you feel bad about yourself. Only you and God have the permission to do that." From that moment on, Diane saw Carol and future Carols from a completely different perspective. Carol was a bully trying to use intimidation as a weapon. Each time Diane faced a "Carol," she remembered the words of that wise physician who gave her the courage to believe in herself.

In retrospect, Diane could see how her behaviors may have made her an enticing target to Carol. As a new nurse, Diane had been so nervous that she had had trouble looking people of authority in the eye, apologized for everything (even things that weren't her fault), and kept admitting her lack of experience in nursing. Some of the nurses took Diane under their wings and helped her to gain the confidence she needed, but to Carol, Diane was the weakest of the bunch. Carol stumbled upon an opportunity to bully someone and took it.

> *We gain strength, and courage, and confidence by each experience in which we really stop to look fear in the face . . . we must do that which we think we cannot.*
>   ~ Eleanor Roosevelt

Bully Attractor: Displaying Passive Behavior and Communication Style

As humans, we each have a natural primary communication style. The four common communication styles are as follows:

1. Assertive
2. Aggressive
3. Passive-aggressive
4. Passive

Assertive Communication

Although all the styles of communication are effective in certain situations, assertive communication is the most effective overall because it demonstrates respect for all parties in an interaction. People displaying assertive communication clearly state their opinions without violating the rights of others, acknowledge that both they and others are valuable, and seek to establish mutually satisfying solutions. People displaying assertive communication use phrases such as the following:

- "How can we solve this problem?"

- "In my opinion . . . ."

- "I'm not comfortable with . . . ."

- "In order to perform well, I need . . . ."

- "Thank you for sharing your perspective. My perspective is different in the following ways . . . ."

- "Although we disagree on some things, let's agree to make patient safety our top priority."

AGGRESSIVE COMMUNICATION

Aggressive communication involves force and manipulation. People displaying aggressive communication attempt to use coercion to get what they want from others. They express their opinions in ways that violate the rights of others, and they have difficulty validating other people's points of view. People displaying aggressive communication use phrases such as the following:

- "I don't care what you have to say."

- "You have to . . . ."

- "I want . . . ."

- "You're wrong . . . ."

- "You are to blame . . . ."

- "That's a stupid idea."

Habitually aggressive communicators naturally engage in overt bullying because their style of communication degrades the opinions of others. The behavior is overt because anyone witnessing the behavior will describe it in a similar way. Aggressive communicators not only use phrases that degrade others, they also display aggressive vocal and body language, like yelling and pointing fingers. Aggressive communicators also interrupt others and dominate conversations.

PASSIVE-AGGRESSIVE COMMUNICATION

Passive-aggressive communicators appear mild mannered and agreeable on the outside but are aggressive on the inside. People displaying the passive-aggressive communication style avoid direct confrontation, express anger subtly, and use facial expressions that don't always match how they feel. Passive-aggressive communicators use phrases such as the following:

- "Oh, I thought you knew . . . ."
- "Can't you take a joke?"
- "I don't understand why you're getting so upset."
- "I was only teasing. What's the big deal?"
- "I meant to accomplish that task. I just forgot."

Passive-aggressive communicators may deliberately or inadvertently engage in covert bullying. In an effort to avoid confrontation, a passive-aggressive communicator may express anger or dislike by withholding information or invitations, and/or by acting friendly to someone's face before speaking disparagingly behind that person's back. Not all passive-aggressive communicators are conscious covert bullies. Some people are habitually passive-aggressive in style because they have not learned how to communicate using the other styles.

PASSIVE COMMUNICATORS

For passive communicators, keeping conflict at bay is a high priority. People displaying a passive communication style avoid expressing their opinions, do not respond openly or directly to hurtful situations, and try to avoid conflict by sitting on both sides of the fence. People who are habitually passive communicators may have a strong desire for everyone to get along or may otherwise not feel comfortable asserting their own needs and desires. People displaying passive communication use phrases such as the following:

- "It doesn't matter to me. Whatever everyone else wants is fine."

- "It's no big deal."

- "I don't want to cause any trouble."

- "I'm sorry."

- "I'll defer to the group."

- "What do YOU think is the best solution?"

People who demonstrate passive communication not only use phrases that seem to give others priority over themselves, they also display passive vocal and body language, like speaking softly and avoiding prolonged eye contact.

People who display passive behavior are more likely than others to become targets of bullies because their behaviors lead bullies to think they are unlikely to fight back. Remember, bullies look for opportunities and easy targets. Unfortunately, from a bully's point of view, individuals who communicate passively appear weak, no matter what the reality.

Is Passive Communication Behavior Putting You at Risk?

Read the following questions and choose the response that best matches your communication style:

1. You are the charge nurse on a busy telemetry unit and just posted the new schedule. A staff member complains to you that the schedule is unfair and that she is working too many weekends. Your response is closest to which of the following?

   a. Vehemently agree with her and tell her you'll discuss the issue with the unit director immediately. Then you don't say anything.

   b. Say nothing because this co-worker complains all the time and you do not wish to encourage her.

   c. Tell her to "take it or leave it."

   d. Suggest that this co-worker discuss the schedule with the unit director.

2. Your unit director is asked to create a bulletin board highlighting the newest CPR guidelines. He assigns that project to you and you create a dynamic bulletin board. You overhear this unit director taking full credit for your work. Your response is closest to which of the following?

   a. Confront the unit director in the hallway so that the entire staff can hear the encounter.

   b. Do nothing. It is really no big deal.

   c. Complain to the staff and say nothing to the unit director.

   d. Ask the unit director for a private conversation to discuss your concerns.

The person who chooses option "b" in either case is demonstrating passive behavior.

Individuals who display passive behavior are more likely to communicate using the following verbal and non-verbal communication techniques:

- Issue extreme apologetic statements
- Speak in general rather than specific terms
- Look away or down when talking to others
- Minimize the seriousness of a hurtful situation
- Use hedge words such as "kinda," "a little," "sort of"
- Speak little, and rarely express opinions, expectations or feelings

People demonstrating passive behaviors use these strategies to avoid conflict, often even if this means compromising their values. They are peacekeepers and can easily be taken advantage of by others.

For example, Dottie had been a nurse for over 30 years. She was sweet, kind, and never said, "No" to anyone. However, when an aggressive nurse started on the unit, it seemed that Dottie was struggling. She became more quiet than usual, couldn't seem to get her work done on time, and frequently appeared distracted. When asked if everything was okay, Dottie always replied with a smile, "Everything is wonderful." When asked if she needed help, she always said, "No, thank you," and insisted she was fine.

One day the aggressive charge nurse gave Dottie a horrible assignment. Two patients needed preparation for the OR, one of which was in isolation and needed to be suctioned every hour. A third patient assigned to Dottie was in four-point leather restraints, requiring Q15 minute vital signs. Dottie never said a

word, even though a few of the nurses ending their shift suggested she ask to change her assignment. Dottie neither asked
for help nor confronted the charge nurse about the assignment.
She just quietly tried to keep up with the insurmountable
demands. She spent three hours charting after her shift was
over. The next day Dottie called off sick.

Dottie's passive behavior and communication style didn't
necessarily mean she lacked confidence or self-esteem. Her
communication style, however, was ineffective in relationship
to an aggressive nurse. The nurse bully in this situation read
Dottie's passive responses as an invitation to bully her.

Dottie was, in fact, a confident professional who needed to
learn to display assertive behaviors in response to an aggressive
nurse. How could Dottie have used assertive communication to
address the issues with the aggressive charge nurse? By "walking tall," looking the charge nurse directly in the eye and saying, "I'm concerned that the assignment you gave me is unsafe
for the patients. What can we do to resolve this?"

Hindsight is always 20/20. If you want to learn to communicate more assertively, begin by reflecting on situations
you've found yourself in where you displayed passive behavior.
Then script the experience using assertive communication.
Rehearse your lines. As with any skill, the more you practice
assertive communication, the better you'll become.

As you practice, remember that assertive communication
always focuses on presenting facts and addressing behaviors,
not blaming, accusing, or attacking a person. You'll find more
examples and sample assertive responses to difficult situations
in future chapters.

BULLY ATTRACTOR: WALKING A DIFFERENT PATH

Even if you are competent and confident in your skills, you can find yourself a target of a bully just because you are different from the rest of the group. Some nurses, despite a high level of accomplishment and confidence, find themselves the target of bullying from the other nurses with whom they work. Unattractive as it is, this type of mob mentality can develop on a unit where nurses within the group gang up on the nurse who is different. It always reminds me of the Mr. Rogers song, "One of these things is not like the other . . . ." However, unlike children enjoying a simple song, these nurses can be mean and destructive to the "outsider."

Although there are many ways someone can be different, the most common involve different degrees, different geographic origins, different ethnic backgrounds, and different genders.

> *Any deviation is looked upon as a perversion, is feared, and is usually a target of hatred and prejudice.*
>
> ~ Joey Skaggs

DIFFERENT DEGREES

The differing entry points into nursing often create tension among a group of nurses. According to an ANA report, published in 2004, 52% of nurses have either a diploma or associate's degree while only 35% of all nurses have a BSN degree. Since all RN program graduates must past the NCLEX examination to obtain a license, many nurses assume it doesn't matter what degree a nurse has. In reality, the NCLEX examination is to ensure the basics of patient care and safety; it's the bare minimum deemed safe for licensure.

This difference in nursing degrees can create jealousy and unhealthy competition in the workplace. It pits the diploma/associate's degree nurses against the BSN nurses and vice versa. I've been witness to student nurses from a BSN program complaining they've been partnered with a working associate's degree nurse during a clinical rotation. Likewise, I've seen a unit of diploma/associate's degree nurses gang up on nurses with BSN or higher degrees. When a nurse pursues a masters or doctorate degree, that nurse's accomplishments are often met with jealousy, competition, and bullying. This is particularly true when the nurse's boss has a lesser degree.

Patricia's first job after attaining her BSN from a respected university was working in a community hospital in her hometown. Patricia wanted to spend a few years at home so she could pay off student loans before moving to a large city. The majority of the nurses on the unit where Patricia started had a diploma or associate's degree, including Patricia's boss. The first day of work, her preceptor and two other nurses approached and said, "Just because you have a big fancy degree from a big fancy school doesn't mean you're better than we are."

Patricia, shocked, hoped they were kidding. Throughout the next few months, however, Patricia frequently received the toughest assignments and once overheard the charge nurse say, "She's the big shot with the big shot degree. This should be easy for her." None of the staff members would help Patricia when she needed it; during report they would leave out important information; when confronted would comment that they assumed since Patricia had a bachelor's degree (mocking) that she could figure it out. After six months, Patricia quit and found a job working with other BSN prepared nurses in a larger hospital. Patricia's problem with bullying ended as she worked among her BSN colleagues. This solution, however, came at a high cost to both Patricia and the smaller hospital.

A nurse can become a target if he or she decides to go back to school at any level. Many nurses don't tell their co-workers about education plans for fear they will now become a target and be criticized.

For example, Wendy always knew she wanted to get her BSN. She worked her way through her associate's program as a single mom and was thrilled to graduate top in her class and get her first job as a registered nurse. However, Wendy wanted to become an educator and knew she would have to advance her degree, starting with her BSN.

Since Wendy had witnessed the harassment other nurses who chose to go back to school received, she decided to keep her acceptance into a local university a secret. To further hide her schooling, she chose not to apply for tuition reimbursement so that even her boss, who had an associate's degree, wouldn't know. Even when Wendy got her degree, she celebrated in silence, not telling anyone what she had accomplished until she left her position for a new job on a new unit where advanced education was supported.

DIFFERENT GEOGRAPHIC AREA

Laura graduated from nursing school during a time when new nurses had trouble finding jobs. When offered a job in another state, Laura gladly packed up her two kids and moved three states away from home, hoping to start her career as a professional nurse in a premier health center. Laura, from a northern state, was moving to the south. She was looking forward to a new fresh start.

Laura wasn't prepared, however, for the bullying she faced just because of her geographic origin. Right from the beginning, the other nurses referred to Laura as "the Yankee." After a few months, it went from "Yankee" to "Damn Yankee" and finally "Goddamn Yankee." Laura wasn't invited to unit social events, was excluded from staff celebrations such as birthdays and weddings, and always took breaks alone.

Interestingly, Laura wasn't shy. She was an extrovert who had no problem standing up for herself. Although new to nursing, Laura was confident in her skills. She had worked in the medical field for 15 years prior to becoming a nurse and was comfortable in a healthcare environment.

Eventually, Laura asked to meet with the unit manager to share her experiences with the staff. Her manager justified the other nurses' behavior by saying that they were just "teasing" Laura and she should learn to take a joke. Her recommendation to Laura was to lighten up a bit and not take things so personally.

Although Laura tried to ignore the bullying behavior, she made the choice to quit after one year, and when a job opened in her hometown, she took it. Although Laura had liked the work she did in the south, she was not willing to work in an environment where bullying behavior based on geographic origin was tolerated.

What if . . .

Laura's unit director had supported her by addressing unprofessional behavior? What if one of Laura's co-workers had defended Laura in front of the bullies? What difference might either of these actions have made to Laura and the hospital that employed her?

DIFFERENT ETHNIC BACKGROUND

Obvious differences in race or culture always present opportunities for conflict. These differences are more apparent in regions of the country where there is a primary group. In western Pennsylvania, where I live, the population is predominately white. In southern California there are many more Latin Americans, and in the south, African Americans. These differences can create situations where members of a minority race may be seen as different and therefore susceptible to bullying.

Marites was born in the Philippines but moved to the United States when she was 10 years old. She graduated from nursing school in Southern California and accepted her first job as a nurse, working on a medical surgical unit in Portland, Oregon. Marites had tried to secure a job in her hometown of San Diego without success.

On Marites' first day, she noticed she was the only Philippine-appearing nurse on her unit. Immediately, Marites felt different. The other nurses, who were primarily white, stared at her and didn't smile. During Marites' first week, a group of nurses approached her and asked if "people from her country" really ate dogs and cats. Marites didn't know what to say.

Throughout the next few months, Marites found printed racial jokes taped to her locker, was repeatedly referred to as someone who ate dogs, and was excluded from any social activities on the unit. After six months, Marites quit, returned home and found a job working with other Filipino nurses.

What if . . .

Instead of the nurses making fun of Marites because of her heritage, they had embraced the opportunity to learn about a different culture? What could they have learned from Marites that would help them to grow personally and professionally?

Different Gender

Nursing, as you know, is a female-dominated profession. Although we are starting to see an increase in the number of male nurses, they represent less than 10% of the total nursing workforce. Male nurses starting a new job on a unit comprised of primarily women can quickly find themselves the targets of bullying. Some nurses don't think men belong in the profession and, therefore, will undermine everything they do.

When Erik started as a new nurse, the other nurses teased him excessively. He was young, cute, blond, and blue-eyed, and really did resemble a Ken doll. Erik was also very polite and soft-spoken (demonstrating a passive communication style). Several of the middle-aged nurses actually started calling Erik "Ken" and thought it was cute to pinch his butt or to whistle at him as he walked down the hall. Erik told me that although he received compliments most of his life on his good looks, he had never felt so stupid and like a sex object until he became a nurse. When asked why he didn't say something, his reply was that he did, but the nurses laughed and started teasing him more.

Make Yourself Less Attractive as a Target

If you have recognized yourself in any descriptions of styles or individuals who are attractive as targets to bullies, the key is to understand what behaviors are attractive to a bully and eliminate them as much as possible. Obviously, you can't change your gender, your geographic origin, or your ethnic roots. You can, however, learn to display confidence even when you don't feel it. You can also build your skills in assertive communication, even if this is not your primary style. The things you can do will help you to prepare for situations in which a bully launches an attack around something you cannot change. Also, the more you display confidence and communicate assertively, the less likely the bully is to pick you as a target in the first place.

Although we have more to say about bullies and what motivates them, we can now identify some fundamental actions to decrease your chances of being chosen as a target of a bully. Draw on your moral courage and commit to anti-bully behaviors:

- Look people in the eye when you talk to them

- Walk tall with your shoulders back and head held high

- Insist upon expressing your opinions as well as listening to the opinions of others

- Check your volume. If you tend to speak softly, raise the volume

- Avoid apologizing unless you have a genuinely good reason to

- Avoid taking responsibility to create harmony, especially at your own expense

- Review the assertive communication behaviors and practice speaking assertively

- Speak with pride about your heritage

This is a beginning list of actions to reduce your appeal as a target for a bully. Keep reading! Future chapters will provide you with more specific strategies to avoid becoming a victim and to ward off bully attacks.

CHAPTER 4

LAYING THE FOUNDATION TO PROTECT YOURSELF

> *Human capacity is equal to human cruelty, and it's up to each of us to tip the balance.*
>
> ~ Alice Walker

As we saw in Chapter 3, bullies are attracted to people who demonstrate behaviors that lead the bully to believe the target will be vulnerable and unlikely to stand up for himself or herself. Bullies are especially attracted to people whose behaviors display diminished self-confidence, demonstrate passive behavior, or walk a different path from the group. An effective bully-proofing strategy involves creating the perception that you are confident, assertive, and prepared to stand up for yourself in the face of differences. This chapter will break down these strategies into specific behaviors.

BULLY-PROOF STRATEGY 1: PROJECT SELF-CONFIDENCE—NO MATTER HOW YOU FEEL

To protect yourself from being an attractive target to a bully, you need to look as though you are confident even though you may not be in a specific situation. In Chapter 3, we explored how looking people in the eye and walking tall creates an impression of self-confidence. Dressing professionally, voicing your opinion, and acting "as if" also create an impression of confidence. The more of these behaviors you adopt, the stronger the sense of self-confidence you'll project. Let's look at each behavior more closely.

Look People in the Eye

In U.S. culture, a person who doesn't look others in the eye is perceived as shy or insecure. When a bully is ranting and raving, spewing venom, the victim typically looks away, avoids eye contact, and displays passivity. That is just the reaction a bully loves!

To minimize your likelihood of becoming a target, make a habit of looking people in the eye when you talk to them. Eye contact communicates a sense of competence and confidence, creating the impression that you are not an easy target.

If an overt bully yells at you, respond by looking the bully directly in the eye. Don't blink. Just make and hold eye contact. A nurse who bullies is not used to getting an "eye challenge" and may back down. You may feel very uncomfortable at first, but keep maintaining eye contact until the bully stops. Looking directly in a bully's eyes during your conversation sends a very clear message that you are not somebody who will put up with his or her shenanigans.

Walk Tall

As we have already discussed, "walking tall," with head held high and shoulders back can help you appear strong and confident rather than weak and vulnerable. Before you walk into a new environment, take a moment to adjust your posture. Stand as tall as you can with your chin up, shoulders back, and eyes looking forward. It also helps if you smile slightly as you walk. Also, make it a habit to "sit tall" rather than slouching in meetings and at the nurses' station. This gives the impression you are confident, secure, and happy. A bully will notice your signals and may assume you aren't an easy target.

DRESS PROFESSIONALLY

The clothes you wear at work send a message. They might say you are proud of your body (low cut shirt, tight fitting uniform); you are conservative and serious (starched white uniform); or you are just going through the motions (dirty, wrinkled uniform). Bullies look for nurses whose dress suggests they are timid, shy, and lack self-confidence. To counter this perception, follow these simple tips:

- FOLLOW THE DRESS CODE POLICY
  Whether it's all white or all blue, make sure you adhere to the policy. You may want to stretch the boundaries because "everyone else does," but don't succumb. Be the ultimate professional and stick to the policy.

- WEAR PATIENT POPULATION APPROPRIATE ATTIRE
  Unless you work in pediatrics, wearing cartoon characters on your uniform can send a message that you are not to be taken seriously, that you are child-like. A bully will spot this and may assume you are an easy target. Instead, make sure your clothing, uniform or not, sends a message of confidence specific to the population you serve.

- DRESS FOR SUCCESS

  Make sure your clothing is clean, without wrinkles, and in good repair. I've seen nurses with holes in their scrub pants, dirty white shoes, and wrinkled lab coats. Sloppy dress sends a message that you aren't serious versus a nurse whose clothing looks professional. Sloppy dress can also give the impression that you are preoccupied or out of control of your life. Dressing this way appeals to bullies because they assume if you are unkempt or out of control, you'll be less likely to challenge them. Clean, professional dress gives the impression that you are serious about your job and in control of life's details.

VOICE YOUR OPINION

In western culture, those who take up "floor space" in meetings and conversations are perceived as strong. Those who remain silent or seldom voice their opinions are perceived as weak or subservient.

For various reasons, some individuals naturally hold back their opinions. Individuals who are introverted are often comfortable holding their opinions inside. They also tend to take longer to process information and prefer to hold back until they have clarified their thinking. Some individuals from non-western cultures do not perceive the give and take of conversations in the same way as U.S. born individuals do. Whatever the cause, a person who does not participate equally in conversations can appear passive and vulnerable—an easy target. Make the effort to verbalize your opinions and share what you know.

> *I don't possess a lot of self-confidence. I'm an actor so I simply act confident every time I hit the stage.*
>
> ~ Arsenio Hall

ACT "AS IF"

Even the most competent person's confidence can be shaken in certain circumstances. When someone performs a task or procedure for the first time, changes positions, goes back to school, or reaches beyond his or her comfort zone, that person's self-confidence tends to take a dip. Bullies know this and may use such vulnerable moments as opportunities to attack. The key is to not let a bully see the temporary vulnerability. How? By acting "as if."

Anytime you find yourself in a situation in which you are less than confident, pretend that you are or act "as if" you have done the job or task in question a million times. For example, starting a new job in a higher position can shake anyone's self-confidence. Although you may have been competent and confident in your previous role, taking on a new position with different skills and greater responsibilities can make you feel like a novice again. It's okay to identify the skills you need to learn and even ask for help, but in the process, act "as if" you are confident you can master the skills quickly.

Once David got through his first few years as a new nurse, he thought his vulnerability was forever gone. Boy was he wrong. Throughout his career, each time David started a new position or got a promotion, the insecurities surfaced and once again he found himself apologizing for his lack of knowledge, avoiding direct eye contact, and being slow to offer his opinion—all passive behaviors. It really wasn't until David started to believe he was capable of learning any new skill that he started to display confidence.

The best protection you have against bullies is your own sense of self-confidence. It's like a magic shield that protects you from the landmines you may step on throughout your career. Even when you aren't feeling self-confident, however, you can choose behaviors that minimize your chances of becoming a target:

- Look people in the eye
- Dress the part of a professional
- Voice your opinion
- Act "as if"

These behaviors have a multiplying effect: the more of them you adopt, the stronger your impression of confidence. The more you display these behaviors, the less attractive you are to a typical bully.

BULLY-PROOF STRATEGY 2: PRACTICE ASSERTIVE BEHAVIOR/COMMUNICATION

In nursing school you learn about body systems, disease processes, treatments, evidence-based practice, and even the art and science of caring. However, it is rare to find courses on effective communication as part of the curriculum. Yet nurses work in high-stress, demanding, and complex environments involving life and death situations that depend on skillful communication between healthcare providers. Add a few bullies into the mix, and even the most articulate person can get quickly derailed and mute. Even if a nurse is strong clinically, weak communication skills may leave that nurse vulnerable to bully attacks.

In Chapter 3, we discussed the four communication styles: assertive, aggressive, passive-aggressive, and passive. The most effective bully-proof form of communication is the assertive style. This style enables you to express yourself with confidence, allows you to deflect negative comments, and minimizes the bully's impact. Assertiveness is not a personality trait. It's a set of communication behaviors that allow professionals to work together to achieve common goals. Except in unsafe or very unimportant situations, assertive communication is the healthiest and preferred communication style in healthcare.

Following is a list of assertive communication behaviors, with examples. Each behavior makes the communicator appear stronger and more difficult as a target. Each behavior works together with the others in powerful ways to prevent bullying. Since no one learns assertive communication overnight, it makes sense to work on one assertive behavior at a time until you've mastered the set. Assertive communication behaviors include the following:

USES COOPERATIVE WORDS

Speaks in terms of "we," "together," and "us" rather than competitive or blaming words, "I" and "you":

> **Cooperative:** "How can we work together for the good of the patient even when we don't agree?"

> **Cooperative:** "Let's listen to everyone's point of view before deciding."

> **Blaming:** "You always ignore my point of view."

> **Blaming:** "I'm sick of your bossy behavior."

DISPLAYS AN EVEN, CONFIDENT VOICE

Speaks in a volume that is neither excessively loud nor soft

GIVES SPECIFIC DESCRIPTIONS

Provides facts and measurable descriptions rather than vague or generalized proclamations:

> **Specific:** "Lois, for the last four days, you've assigned me four patients while the other nurses on the unit were assigned only three."

> **Specific:** "I could hear you yelling at the nurses' station all the way down the hall."

> **Vague:** "Lois, you always assign me an unfair workload!"

> **Vague:** "You are always yelling."

USES OPEN/HONEST STATEMENTS

Describes feelings and concerns in straightforward ways:

> **Straightforward:** "I'm concerned that patient safety will be compromised . . . ."

> **Straightforward:** "I'm not comfortable with . . . ."

> **Straightforward:** "It's unfair and unprofessional to criticize me in front of patients. If you want to discuss my performance, please do so in private."

> **Not straightforward:** "How do others think we should handle this?"

> **Not straightforward:** "If you think that's best, I guess I could manage. . . ."

> **Not straightforward:** Silence in the face of disagreement.

ACTIVELY LISTENS

Demonstrates openness to and respect for others' opinions:

Listening: Looks person in the eye

Listening: Positions self at the same level of person speaking (either sitting or standing)

Listening: Refrains from interrupting

Listening: Acknowledges other person's point of view

Not listening: Allows eyes to wander while the other is speaking

Not listening: Places self in dominate or threatening body position

Not listening: Interrupts

Not listening: Ignores or discounts other person's point of view

FOCUSES ON THE ISSUE, NOT THE PERSON

Maintains professionalism and diffuses emotional and defensive responses by sticking to facts over personal attacks:

Focus on the issue: "The problem is . . . ."

Focus on the issue: "Let's focus on the issue, not on . . . ."

Focus on the issue: "Is this what's best for our patients?"

Focus on the person: "You're not listening!"

Focus on the person: "We wouldn't have this problem if you weren't so stubborn."

Focus on the person: "We only have these problems when you are working."

Uses Non-Judgmental Communication

Maintains professionalism and diffuses emotional and defensive responses with non-judgmental verbal and non-verbal language. Demonstrates relaxed posture and refrains from finger-pointing:

Non-judgmental: "Help me to understand why . . . ."

Judgmental: "You don't know what you are talking about."

Actively Communicates Expectations as well as Sets Boundaries

Communicates needs and expectations proactively and assertively; avoids suppressing needs and opinions to please others:

Communicating expectations: "When you are late for your shift, I have difficulty getting home to get my kids on the bus on time. I need you to get to work on time."

Communicating boundaries: "That solution seems unfair to me. Let's generate some other possibilities."

Communicating boundaries: "I am willing to do . . . ."

Not communicating: Keeping silent about expectations; allowing others to set boundaries without equal input.

NEGOTIATES, BARGAINS, AND COMPROMISES

Seeks to resolve problems and disagreements rather than allow them to fester; participates in generating and evaluating options:

> **Negotiating:** "What are our options for solving this problem?"

> **Negotiating:** "How can we compromise?"

> **Negotiating:** "What alternatives do we have?"

> **Negotiating:** "Let's figure out a way to . . . ."

> **Not negotiating:** Keeping silent in discussions about matters that directly affect you; allowing others to make decisions without equal input.

REFUSES TO ACCEPT DEMEANING TREATMENT

Interrupts disrespectful tirades and addresses unfair behavior:

> **Refusing demeaning treatment:** "I'll be happy to continue this discussion when you stop yelling."

> **Refusing demeaning treatment:** "Please allow me to finish giving my opinion without interruption. I'll extend the same courtesy to you."

> **Accepting demeaning treatment:** Keeping silent in the face of insults, interruptions, and other bullying behavior.

Valerie was a new educator in the department. Some of the other educators developed a habit of giving Valerie a lecture to do at the last minute. They consistently had excuses as to why they couldn't do the lectures as scheduled. Although the other educators asked nicely and always thanked her, Valerie suspected they were dumping on her. Valerie felt overwhelmed and frustrated but always said, "Sure" and then did her best. When she found out that Marie, after dumping a last-minute lecture on her, was seen in the cafeteria enjoying a leisurely lunch, Valerie knew she needed to change her response the next time. Valerie summoned her moral courage and made a plan.

Two weeks later, Marie flew into Valerie's office, begging her to do her cardiac lecture starting in 30 minutes. Valerie looked Marie in the eye and assertively said, "I will gladly do any lectures you need me to do when you give me at least one day's notice. I am not able to help you today." Marie asked several more times, but Valerie stuck to her guns. When Valerie communicated her one-day rule and consistently held to it, the other educators stopped coming to her with "emergencies."

Valerie wasn't a naturally assertive communicator, but she learned to communicate this way when needed. When she realized Marie was unfairly asking her to do lectures, Valerie thought about how she would handle the next lecture "emergency." She wrote down her ideal response and practiced it over and over until it felt more natural. When the time came, she was able to communicate in an assertive manner with Marie. Over time, Valerie learned how to be more assertive in other aspects of her work life and felt that she had more control over her time.

If you, like Valerie, are not naturally assertive, you can learn to use assertive communication as a skill. You may be uncomfortable with your first attempts, but with practice, assertive communication behaviors can become effective tools in your workplace toolbox.

People who fail to learn to communicate assertively sometimes become so frustrated with how others treat them that they vacillate between passive and aggressive communication behavior, neither of which is effective with bullies.

> *The basic difference between being assertive and being aggressive is how our words and behavior affect the rights and well-being of others.*
>
> ~ Sharon Anthony Bower

ADDITIONAL STRATEGIES TO PRACTICE ASSERTIVENESS

ENGAGE IN POSITIVE SELF-THOUGHTS AND SELF-TALK

Your internal dialogue can have a profound effect on your external dialogue. There is a connection between what you think and what you say and do. Work to fill your thoughts with positive self-talk. Recount your strengths and accomplishments. Remind yourself that you CAN respond effectively to difficult situations. The more time you spend building yourself up internally and thinking about successfully confronting a bully, the more likely you are to succeed. Visualize yourself speaking assertively and having a positive outcome.

REHEARSE YOUR RESPONSE

Once you understand the assertive communication style, script a few responses to negative situations you commonly encounter. Then practice saying your lines. Like an actor, the more you practice your lines, the more comfortable you will be during the performance.

When Jan was promoted to a corporate director level position, one of the chief nursing officers (CNO) openly criticized and refused to participate in a new program Jan had developed. The CNO attacked Jan personally even though the program was a system initiative and not Jan's personal project. The attack happened during a meeting in front of many leaders, and Jan was mortified.

After the meeting, Jan's boss pulled her aside and suggested Jan speak to the CNO about her behavior. Jan couldn't imagine actually initiating a conversation with this woman, especially after her public attack. However, Jan's boss said the key to her success was to learn the skill of assertive communication and to recognize situations that needed to be addressed, not ignored. This was one of those situations.

To help Jan prepare, her boss suggested writing down what she wanted to say, actually scripting the conversation. Jan's boss then recommended she practice over and over again and speak to the CNO within 48 hours. This would give Jan enough time to practice and to let go of some of the emotions involved.

Jan chose a phone call as her communication channel. With Jan's script in front of her, she took a deep breath, summoned her moral courage, and dialed the phone. The conversation started out like this:

"Hi, Peggy. Would you be open to having a conversation with me about the meeting yesterday?" The CNO indicated a willingness to discuss the meeting.

Jan continued, "When you raised your voice, pointed your finger at me, and criticized the program, I felt as though you were personally attacking me."

The CNO apologized and said she had been meaning to call Jan about her behavior. The CNO explained why she behaved as she had and how it had nothing to do with the program or Jan.

The reason she had "attacked" Jan was because she was angry about being forced to do something whether she wanted to do it or not. The CNO's anger was really directed at somebody else; Jan just got caught in the crossfire. The CNO thanked Jan for calling and complimented her on how professionally Jan handled the situation.

Jan was relieved and felt good knowing she had pushed through her discomfort and communicated assertively. She was able to establish a good relationship with the CNO for the remainder of their working relationship.

If the CNO were a hard-core bully, of course, her response may have been different. However, assertiveness is a vital communication skill in all professional situations and worth the effort to learn. Often, an assertive approach is enough to get another person to consider the appropriateness and the impact of his or her behavior on others.

Practice using assertive communication on relatively benign and easier situations before using it on a queen bully! Review the assertive response examples given in this chapter. Engage in positive thoughts; envision your success. Rehearse your response until you can say it clearly and firmly.

> *Respect your efforts, respect yourself. Self-respect leads to self-discipline. When you have both firmly under your belt, that's real power.*
>
> ~ Clint Eastwood

BULLY-PROOF STRATEGY 3: BE PREPARED FOR ISSUES SURROUNDING DIFFERENCES

Knowing that being different puts you at risk for being the target of a bully allows you to be prepared. Some differences are obvious: ethnic background, gender, accent, etc. But others are less obvious: going back to school, getting a promotion, worshipping differently, holding a different political affiliation, etc. Anything that can be viewed as a difference can be attractive to the bully. It gives the bully a focal point for attack.

In any situation where you have an obvious difference that a bully criticizes or pokes fun at, do not respond with silence. Name the criticism and bring the focus back to the work. This is an assertive communication behavior that works well with criticism or joking surrounding differences.

Consider these responses:

- NEW HAIRCUT
  "What does my hair have to do with patient care?"

- ADVANCED DEGREE
  "Is there a reason that you mention my degree as part of our conversation about our patients?"

- DIFFERENT ETHNICITY
  "How does the color of my skin affect the work at hand?"

- GENDER DIFFERENCE
  "Help me to understand what my being male has to do with this project."

- GENDER DIFFERENCE
  "I don't find jokes about my gender funny or relevant to patient care. Let's focus on the job we are here to do."

- DIFFERENT GEOGRAPHIC ORIGIN
  "How does the place I came from have anything to do with our job as nurses?"

Some differences, of course, are not obvious. There may be times when you decide to hide your differences; you don't have to share your personal beliefs or political views. However, there are times when others know these differences.

For example, let's say you've decided to advance your degree but you know the existing nurses in your department will give you a hard time. You've heard them openly criticize others by saying, "A BSN is a waste of your time." "Oh, you think you're a big shot now because you have more letters after your name." While you don't have to advertise your decision to continue your schooling, your colleagues may discover your plans anyway. You shouldn't have to hide your educational efforts or forgo tuition reimbursement to avoid bullying.

In these situations, it is still effective to name the inappropriate comment or joke and then turn the focus back to work.

Consider these responses:

- EDUCATION/TRAINING
  "I respect your choice around professional training. I trust you will respect my choice as well. In any case, let's agree to focus on the patients."

- DIFFERENCE IN VIEWPOINT
  "I hear your opinion. My opinion is different than yours. What does this have to do with our patients?"

- POLITICAL DIFFERENCES
  "We may disagree on political matters, but we can agree to strive for excellent patient care. Let's agree to focus on that."

- LIFESTYLE OR ORIENTATION DIFFERENCES
  "Help me to understand how my taste in music (or my
  sexual orientation, or my roots in New Hampshire, or
  my religion) impacts our department."

In every situation in which you are criticized for your differences, address the criticism and redirect the conversation
back to the work. Over time, the bullying will decrease or stop.

Projecting self-confidence and communicating assertively
are skills you can learn. These skills lay the foundation you
need to bully-proof yourself. While you will learn step-by-step
approaches later in this book, the foundational skills themselves
will go a long way toward decreasing bully attacks directed at
you.

Of course, it takes time and practice to master the skills. Try
practicing one behavior at a time, trying things out with friends
and family first. Practice in small, less severe situations before
you try the skills in high-risk situations. Script what you will say
and then practice saying it in front of a mirror. Practicing in
front of a mirror can enable you to view your body language
and make sure you're displaying a confident appearance. With
time and practice, you will begin to use assertive communication phrases without prompting. The behaviors will become
part of your skill set to use when appropriate. Bullies beware!

Let's turn our attention now to the "why" behind the bully
behavior, especially in the nursing profession. Understanding
why nurses bully can help you to identify specific characteristics and behavior patterns seen in the bullies in your workplace. This understanding, in turn, can help you choose effective strategies to neutralize the power of those bullies.

CHAPTER 5

THE "WHY" BEHIND NURSE BULLY BEHAVIOR

> *Some people won't be happy until they've pushed you to the ground. What you have to do is have the courage to stand your ground and not give them the time of day. Hold on to your power and never give it away.*
> ~ Donna Schoenrock

I recently received an e-mail from a newly graduated nurse asking me if she could talk with me about a bullying situation on her unit. Maggie was in her late 40's and had always wanted to be a nurse, but achieving her dream hadn't been possible until after her kids were grown. Maggie went through nursing school and started her first job on a busy medical surgical unit in a tertiary hospital. Maggie knew all about bullying and thought she was prepared. However, when the bullies didn't come in the guise Maggie had expected, she was caught off guard.

The bullies on the unit where Maggie worked weren't the seasoned, "crusty" nurses but young 20-year-olds who had only a few years on the job! These younger nurses perceived themselves to have more experience, more skill, and more authority than an "older, new nurse." Maggie had never felt as humiliated in her life as she did during her first six months on that unit.

Bullies in nursing come in all different shapes and sizes. They can be experienced or inexperienced nurses, male or female. Some bullies wear their "bully medal" like a badge of honor while others hide their bully ways underneath a blanket of sweetness. In the end they all share a common trait: bullies are people who use their perceived power to intimidate or harm those whom they perceive as weaker or threatening.

This chapter will take an in-depth look at bullies and their motivations for bad behavior. Learning to identify underlying characteristics of most bullies will help you protect yourself from the bully.

WHY BULLIES BULLY

Theories about why some nurses bully abound. Here are some of the top contenders:

- Nursing is an oppressed professional group.

- The place of nursing in the healthcare hierarchy creates a sense of powerlessness and helplessness, leading to low self-esteem.

- The gender imbalance in nursing taps into issues of female-to-female competition and aggression.

THEORY 1: NURSING IS AN OPPRESSED PROFESSIONAL GROUP

Not long ago, nurses were viewed as the physician's handmaidens. Nursing was considered a passive occupation and a service position. Nurses gave up their chairs for doctors and didn't even carry stethoscopes. As recently as the early 1900's, a nursing job description included expectations such as maintaining a warm temperature in patient rooms and mopping floors.

Today, a nurse's job description includes conducting advanced disease-specific assessments, coordinating care, promoting safe discharge, using sophisticated equipment, diagnosing illness, and writing prescriptions. Moreover, nurses need to fully comprehend research, regulatory requirements, and healthcare financials. However, despite this advancement in knowledge, competence, and scope of practice, nurses are often still not recognized for the value they bring to the delivery of healthcare.

The continuing perception that nurses are less important than doctors, don't deserve a voice in their work, and need to succumb to the forces of administrative decisions and physician influence can lead nurses to feel inferior. These feelings can manifest in bullying behavior, with nurses "taking it out" on each other. Since nurses can't "take it out" on administrators or physicians, the theory is that they take it out on the already oppressed, subservient group. What's worse is that bully nurses choose the most vulnerable of the group as their targets. This is true horizontal violence.

THEORY 2: A SENSE OF POWERLESSNESS LEADS TO BULLYING

Keys to job satisfaction in nearly every profession include autonomy, recognition, and collaborative practice. The opposite of this is a perception or real lack of decision-making power or influence.

There are more than 3.1 million nurses in this country and only about 650,000 physicians, yet nurses are known as the silent majority. While nurses are held accountable for outcomes, they are still paid by the hour; have to commit to a punch-in and punch-out schedule; and are afforded minimal or no representation at decision-making tables in their workplaces. Feelings of frustration, coupled with an increasingly complex and stressful job, can create an environment where nurses lash out at each other. Becoming a bully helps certain nurses to gain some of the perceived power they are missing in their profession.

Sarah was known as the queen bully on a busy step-down unit. Sarah was openly critical of others, frequently complained about administration, and was adversarial with the physician staff. On outward appearance, Sarah was just mean. Students dreaded being paired with her; nurses hated to be working on the same shift as her; and the unit manager even stopped allowing Sarah to act as a preceptor for new nurses.

A few nurses who worked on another unit had attended nursing school with Sarah 30 years earlier. These nurses insisted that Sarah didn't start out mean. In fact, Sarah was respectful, pleasant, loved having students with her, and was fun to be around.

However, Sarah initially worked in an environment where the other nurses constantly criticized her and where physicians were known to throw temper tantrums and charts across the unit. When she complained about physician behavior to the unit manager, Sarah was told to "toughen up" and that since the physicians made the money, Sarah would just have to deal with them.

When Sarah complained about the nurses openly criticizing her in front of others (even patients), the manager somehow twisted the information to imply Sarah was wrong and the other nurses were right.

Over time, Sarah stopped trying to improve things; she just gave up. She told one of her friends that the only defense is a good offense and since she had no say in anything, why should she even try to make things better? Sarah became bitter about her job and bitter about nursing. Instead of leaving a toxic environment, however, Sarah stayed and became a bully.

THEORY 3: THE NURSING PROFESSION TAPS INTO FEMALE-TO-FEMALE AGGRESSION

For centuries, females have competed against each other to catch the right mate. Books and movies have long showcased how vindictive and competitive females can be just to get what they want. Think about Scarlet O'Hara's jealousy over the relationship between Ashley and Melanie in the classic, *Gone with the Wind.* Scarlet spent most of her life trying to make herself look better by making Melanie look bad.

Females comprise 90% of the nursing workforce. Theories suggest that age-old female "competition" has shifted from competing over a man to competing over status, respect, and position in the nursing environment. The same behaviors once witnessed between two women fighting over a man are the ones witnessed today in the behavior of bullies. I have heard many women say they would rather work with a department of men than women any day. Perhaps you have said the same. Women can be catty and cruel, yet we allow this bad behavior to continue because, "That's just the way women are."

As mentioned in Chapter 2, Cheryl Dellasega, Ph.D., has studied female-to-female aggression extensively and has written several books on the topic. Dellasega's research on bullying behavior among women shines a light on how relational aggression among females leads to bullying, eating disorders, and conflict. Dellasega's research helps explain why bullying is so prevalent in the female-dominated nursing profession. According to Dellasega, women deal with conflict differently than men. In addition, negative experiences girls have can manifest into bullying behaviors in women.

The "Why" Behind the Behavior

Based on the theories above, we can expect bullies to demonstrate behavior driven by feelings of oppression, powerlessness, and competition, whether those feelings are on the surface or buried deep below. Bully behaviors stem from the need to transfer feelings of anger, resentment, powerlessness, or even fear of rejection, onto somebody else.

The source of a bully's negative feelings, as well as the bully's level of awareness of his or her feelings, will influence how that bully attacks. Understanding why nurses bully can help you to identify specific characteristics and behavior patterns seen in the bullies in your workplace. This understanding, in turn, can help you choose effective strategies to neutralize the power of those bullies.

In general, bullies are good at their jobs and may even be well respected for a particular skill or behavior. Remember Cathy from the opening pages of this book? Cathy was an excellent clinician and well respected for her clinical knowledge. Cathy's unit manager also admired her because Cathy consistently picked up the slack and worked overtime whenever it was available. However, Cathy was a queen bully.

Underlying Characteristics and Driving Forces

As I've mentioned before, whether a bully is a professional nurse at a prestigious hospital or a school-age child on the playground, you can expect to find common characteristics. The current literature identifies three primary underlying issues or habits that characterize most bullies:

1. Issues with self-esteem—low and high
2. Former or current victims of abuse
3. Aggressive or passive-aggressive communication style

> *I'm not concerned with your liking or disliking me. All*
> *I ask is that you respect me as a human being.*
> ~ Jackie Robinson

UNDERLYING ISSUE 1: SELF-ESTEEM—LOW AND HIGH

Self-esteem reflects a person's overall sense of self-worth, abilities, and confidence. A positive sense of self is a basic human requirement. We all require a certain level of self-esteem just to get up in the morning and participate in the workplace. The strength and health of self-esteem varies from person to person, depending upon a number of factors. Personality traits inherited from parents and grandparents, as well as one's experiences encountered throughout childhood and adolescent years, can impact general self-esteem in positive or negative ways.

Looking at self-esteem as it relates to bullies can be complicated. We know that some bullies have a low level of self-esteem and therefore pick on others to make themselves feel better while other bullies have a high level of self-esteem and believe themselves to be superior as well as entitled to certain things. These bullies pick on people they believe to be beneath them.

LOW SELF-ESTEEM

Lack of respect for a female-dominated profession, coupled with the existing hierarchies in healthcare systems, exaggerates feelings of low self-worth and frustration in some nurses. People with low self-esteem have difficulty managing anger and frustration appropriately and tend to lash out at others, typically others they perceive as weaker than themselves.

Individuals with low self-esteem may lack the coping mechanisms to handle negative situations, so they internalize those experiences and then feel bad about themselves. Feeling bad results in emotional and sometimes physical pain. To avoid negative situations where they might feel bad again, individuals with low self-esteem either avoid others or hurt others "before they can get hurt."

Obviously, not all nurses with low self-esteem turn into bullies, but some do. Bullies with low self-esteem tend to minimize others' accomplishments, downplay awards and compliments received by others, and blame everyone else when something goes wrong. Remember, this is all in an attempt to avoid being hurt.

HIGH SELF-ESTEEM

Some new research shows that bullies, especially teenagers, actually have high self-esteem. Bullies in this category have a sense of entitlement and superiority over others, lack compassion, are quick to react, and have limited social skills. These bullies actually enjoy being cruel to others and may even brag about their bad behavior to their friends.

Some believe the excessively high self-image of this category of bully stems from the movement beginning in the 1980's when parents were encouraged to protect their children's self-esteem by overt praise and heightened admiration. These are the parents who insisted that every kid who played a sport got a trophy, whether the kid played well or not. Whatever the cause, some bullies believe they are better and more entitled than others.

Although bullies with excessively high self-esteem can be any age, more of them seem to be in the Millennial/Generation Y group. In healthcare, these are the newer graduate nurses who are now in their 20's. These are the bullies who tormented Maggie, the 40-year-old described at the beginning of this chapter.

In general, Millennials don't have the same struggle with confrontation as the Baby Boomer generation and are not afraid to stand up for themselves if they believe they have been wronged. Of course, not all Millennials are bullies, and not everyone with a high sense of self-esteem is suspect as a bully. Individual nurses who can't balance their heightened sense of self-esteem with appropriate interpersonal skills sometimes turn to bullying.

> *When people don't like themselves very much, they have to make up for it. The classic bully was actually a victim first.*
>
> ~ Tom Hiddleston

UNDERLYING ISSUE 2: FORMER OR CURRENT VICTIMS OF ABUSE

It's not uncommon to find someone who is being victimized at home come to work and victimize others. Some victims of domestic violence perpetuate the cycle of violence by victimizing others, which allows them to compensate for feelings of powerlessness at home.

For example, Joan was a battered wife. Although she never outright admitted it, the evidence was clear. Joan came into work with fresh bruises, small cuts and scrapes, and once even with a broken finger. Her husband frequently called the nurses' station, demanding to talk with Joan. Others could hear him yelling at Joan. Colleagues could see a look of fear and anxiety in Joan's eyes at the mere mention that she had a call from her husband.

Instead of seeking help, Joan resorted to picking on a few of the nurses who were quiet, new, or were floating to the unit for the day. Joan was frequently overheard openly criticizing these nurses, even calling one "stupid." She'd say, "Didn't they teach you anything in nursing school?" Joan didn't have the coping mechanisms to deal with her personal environment of abuse and therefore transferred it to her work environment.

Note: Realizing the bully may have been a victim once or is currently a victim of abuse doesn't excuse bad behavior. No past or present situation gives a person the right to make victims of others.

Underlying Issue 3: Aggressive & Passive-Aggressive Communication Styles

Needless to say, bullies don't typically engage in healthy, respectful dialogue. This may be because they lack skills, desire, or both. Individuals who habitually demonstrate aggressive or passive-aggressive communication behaviors are more likely than others to behave as bullies. An aggressive communicator, by nature, primarily engages in overt bullying, while a passive-aggressive communicator naturally engages in covert behaviors. Both are likely to target individuals who habitually demonstrate passive communication behaviors. In any case, be it perpetrator or victim, communication behaviors are learned, and they can be changed.

Aggressive or Hostile Communication Style

Individuals communicating aggressively express their needs, feelings, and opinions in ways that violate the needs, feelings, and opinions of others. Individuals who use this style as their primary mode of communication tend to be verbally abusive and exhibit overt bullying behaviors. They yell, openly criticize, argue in public, and can even be physically abusive.

Aggressive communication often stems from low or high self-esteem, repressed emotional wounds, and/or feelings of powerlessness. Bullies compensate for these feelings by acting out against others in observable threatening ways. Aggressive communication behaviors you can observe include the following:

- Using sarcasm to make a point
- Placing blame on another person
- Speaking in extremes/generalizations (always/never)
- Raising the voice or shouting
- Using forceful body language, like pointing fingers or invading personal space
- Interrupting frequently; failing to listen to others' points of view
- Demonstrating impatience and low frustration tolerance
- Using "you" statements to blame others
- Reacting quickly and/or impulsively
- Using loud, obnoxious tone and language

Colleagues always knew when Dina was working by the loud outbursts heard throughout the shift. She was well known for getting out of her chair, pointing her finger, and challenging anyone who said or did something she wasn't happy about. Dina's anger was easily triggered by the charge nurse giving her another patient, a physician asking why a patient didn't receive medications, or another nurse telling Dina she had switched chairs.

Dina seemed to revel in letting everyone know when she was unhappy. She also seemed to love to argue and "one-up" everyone. No matter what a colleague did, Dina did it better. No matter how busy her peers were, Dina was busier. Whatever anyone else said, they were wrong and Dina was right. It was exhausting trying to have a simple conversation with Dina. Always looking for a fight, Dina was an extreme example of the aggressive communication style.

Passive-Aggressive Mode of Communication

Individuals demonstrating passive-aggressive communication behaviors appear passive on the outside while they are acting out anger on the inside. These individuals choose subtle and indirect approaches to hostility. These are the people who are as nice as pie to your face but then stab you in the back as soon as you turn around, smiling as they turn the knife. They use guerilla warfare techniques against the enemy. These bullies demonstrate covert categories of behaviors, including the following:

- Talking about people behind their backs
- Failing to take responsibility for negative feedback
- Questioning/judging others in indirect ways
- Failing to honestly share concerns
- Acting in ways inconsistent with words
- Failing to make eye contact
- Exhibiting facial expressions that don't match their feelings (e.g., smiling while angry)

- Feigning helpfulness while withholding help and/or vital information

- Verbally committing to action, then doing nothing

Judy was working 12-hour days and following Sally's shift for consecutive nights. After a busy night, Sally told Judy she hadn't had time to complete the operating room (OR) checklist for the patient scheduled in the OR at 8:00 a.m. and that she hadn't had a chance to bathe her patients or change IV tubing.

When Sally asked Judy if she wanted her to stay to complete the tasks, Judy replied sweetly while smiling, "Oh no. You go home and rest. I have another 12 hours to catch up. See you tonight."

As soon as Sally left, Judy started complaining about her to the other nurses. "Can you believe this big-shot nurse? Not only did she forget to do the OR checklist, bathe the most complicated patient, and change the IV tubing, but she left me dry IV bags and now I have to rehang them all!"

When Sally returned 12 hours later and asked Judy if everything was okay, Judy replied with a smile, "Fine. No problems."

At the end of her shift, however, Judy somehow "forgot" to hang the blood on one patient, didn't draw the labs on another, and just happened to give Kayexelate on another just before leaving (Kayexelate is given to decrease potassium levels and causes significant diarrhea). Another nurse witnessed Judy saying, "Since Sally is a big-shot nurse, let's see how she deals with this."

Judy's passive-aggressive behaviors are common in healthcare. Although Judy appears to be nice, she is a bully. Her style of bullying can be quite dangerous if the target is unaware of the inconsistency between Judy's outward demeanor and her inward anger and intentions.

What if . . .

Judy used assertive communication with Sally and said, "Sally, it's important that you complete your work before you go home. I want you to finish the OR checklist and change the tubing. However, I can ask the nursing assistant to do the baths."

Understanding Bully Behavior Doesn't Equal Accepting It

It's important to understand why bullies bully. However, understanding shouldn't be confused with accepting. The behaviors bullies use are destructive, inappropriate, and wrong, even if the bully has circumstances (a good excuse) that help explain the behaviors. My goal in sharing potential reasons behind bully behavior is to aid you in developing strategies to protect yourself. The more you understand a bully's motivation, and the quicker you can identify the behaviors you are facing (overt or covert), the easier it will be to choose the best strategy to neutralize any bully who targets you.

In Chapter 6, you'll deepen your understanding of bully motives and behavior by learning five classic profiles of bullies. Chances are you'll recognize some nurses you know!

In Chapter 7, you'll use the information you've learned to develop strategies to protect yourself as well as to confront bullying behavior effectively.

PROFILES OF BULLY NURSES YOU MAY KNOW

Now that we've identified the primary reasons behind bullying in the nursing profession, it's time to identify the different types of bullies. Most bullies fit into rough profiles that are easy to recognize. Within the profiles, nurses share similarities that make it easy for you to identify their behaviors and therefore deploy effective defensive tactics. Nurse bullies are nurses you may know either personally or through others. The major profiles are as follows:

- SuperNurse
- EnergyVampire
- ViperNurse
- SororityNurse
- BitterNurse

As you read the descriptions, you may notice that some of the behaviors overlap, and some nurses may fit more than one profile. The important thing is to recognize various overt and covert behaviors so you can respond with defensive tactics.

> *Why was I born with such contemporaries?*
> ~ Oscar Wilde

SuperNurse (Overt)

SuperNurse knows everything, is the best at everything, and reminds you and everyone else of this fact every day. This nurse walks tall, proud of his or her greatness, with shoulders back and head held high. SuperNurse has a bladder made of iron, never has to take a break or go to the bathroom, and thinks you're weak if you do. "Break? You want a break? I haven't taken a break, eaten, or peed in 30 years! You're all pathetic and weak!" SuperNurse refers to the new nurses as "babies." "Look at the new babies who just started. I wonder if they're potty trained yet."

SuperNurse always has to save the day. In a crisis situation this nurse tells everyone to get out of the way while he or she pulls out a cape and sword to save the world. SuperNurse never needs your help because you are an idiot, or worse yet, a baby nurse. Besides, he or she can single-handedly take care of all of the patients because SuperNurse is great!

Even physicians are wary of nurses in this category. Their reputations are well known throughout the hospital; the rumor is that they eat interns as well as new nurses for breakfast.

A classic SuperNurse, Janice never smiled, that is, unless she made one of the new nurses or medical interns cry. Her weapons? Knowledge and a quick, sharp tongue. Janice prided herself on being the smartest, most experienced, and most capable nurse in the universe. When the new nurses started, she stared them down like a drill sergeant during boot camp, asking question after question until the new nurses got one wrong and then said sarcastically, "Great! The new nurses are getting dumber and dumber. I guess I'll have to teach you all how to be real nurses since they didn't teach you anything in nursing school."

Getting Janice as a preceptor was a fate worse than death. Most new nurses only lasted two weeks before they either quit or transferred to another unit. Finally, the unit manager stopped giving Janice new orientees. Janice's response was that the new nurses were cowards and couldn't handle the job.

OVERT BEHAVIORS OF SUPERNURSE

SuperNurse doesn't hide the fact that he or she is a bully. Actually, SuperNurse is proud of his or her bully behaviors and enjoys seeing the victim's reactions. SuperNurse's methods are overt, witnessed and easily identified by others. If you're the target, you know it and so does everyone else.

Public humiliation, intimidation, yelling, and openly criticizing are the primary behaviors used by SuperNurse—all overt and proudly displayed. Even when this nurse employs typically covert behavior, such as rolling his or her eyes, SuperNurse makes sure the victim and others are watching. SuperNurse thrives on audiences, both victim and those who observe. In the mind of SuperNurse, the bigger the audience, the better.

Cathy, from Chapter 1, was a SuperNurse. Everyone knew it, including nurses on her unit and others: students, physicians, interns, and even administrators. Cathy's reputation for eating nurses and interns alive was well known, based on incidents witnessed by many.

ENERGYVAMPIRE (OVERT)

EnergyVampire nurse sucks the life right out of everyone who comes near. He or she constantly complains about everything, even the weather. For example, you say, "It's supposed to be a nice day today."

EnergyVampire replies, "Nice? I hate the warm weather. This just means I'm going to have to start taking care of the yard because my spouse is too damn lazy." EnergyVampire is overtly critical and finds fault with everything and everyone.

For example, during a staff meeting, your boss acknowledges everyone's hard work and rewards the staff by offering a pizza party. While everyone else is thankful, EnergyVampire goes off on a rampage for the rest of the day, complaining, "A pizza party? Is that all we get for our hard work? With all the money this place makes off of our blood, sweat, and tears, we should get a raise instead!"

Negative gossip is EnergyVampire's source of true pleasure—this nurse lives for it! "Hey (smiling), did you hear that Susie got written up for arguing with the family in room 14? You know, Susie is always arguing with family members. I knew it was only a matter of time."

EnergyVampire's mission is to observe any signs of happiness or joy on the unit and deflate them like a balloon until only gloom and doom are left. For instance, you just got engaged and proudly show your engagement ring to the staff. While everyone is gawking over your ring, EnergyVampire says nothing. It's not until this nurse gets you alone that he or she tells you that 55% of all marriages end in divorce, all men cheat, and it's only a matter of time before your beloved turns from Prince Charming to loser. EnergyVampire walks away smiling while you feel like you've been punched in the gut.

OVERT BEHAVIORS OF ENERGYVAMPIRE

EnergyVampire's behaviors can generally be easily observed by others; however, they are at times more subtle than those of SuperNurse. Although EnergyVampire loves to deflate anyone's good mood, he or she tends to find power in smaller groups or individuals, as opposed to SuperNurse who thrives on large audiences.

Bickering, blaming, gossiping, and eye rolling are EnergyVampire's primary bully weapons. These behaviors are observable, but sometimes you don't immediately recognize them as bullying behavior. You might initially think EnergyVampires are miserable human beings who rain on everyone's parade simply because they are so unhappy themselves. Make no mistake about it. EnergyVampires are bullies because they get satisfaction from inflicting gloom on others. EnergyVampires withhold supportive words and behaviors and generally cause disruption in the work environment.

Sarah, from Chapter 5, was an EnergyVampire. After years of working in an unhealthy work environment, she became miserable and angry. Because she never had anything nice to say, she became somebody whom others avoided. Sarah's decision to give up and stop trying to make things better resulted in her becoming extremely unhappy and a negative influence on the unit.

VIPERNURSE (COVERT)

ViperNurse is a silent-but-deadly nurse. ViperNurse is the most dangerous of all bullies because, as with the viper found in nature, you don't even see this bully coming. ViperNurse cultivates friendships, initially offering unwavering support to anyone in need. ViperNurse will praise you in front of others, but be warned: he or she will talk badly about you behind your back. ViperNurse is a back-stabber, and when you least expect it, this nurse will "zing" you. Sometimes it takes years for ViperNurse's covert bullying to be uncovered, but it's always there lurking and waiting for its next victim.

Becky, a young new nurse, became an unsuspecting target of Myra, a classic ViperNurse. Myra was working the night shift and gave report to Becky, who was working the day shift. Myra gave Becky report on a patient who had an a.m. CT scan ordered. When Becky asked Myra if she had taken the patient to radiology for his CT scan, Myra replied that it was the day shift's responsibility to take care of all a.m. CT scans. After all, said Myra, "a.m. occurs during the day." Becky thanked Myra for letting her know.

Whenever Becky worked the night shift over the next few weeks, she left the a.m. CT scans for the day shift. It wasn't long before Becky got called into the boss's office and reprimanded for "dumping" on the day shift. Becky learned that the night shift had responsibility to take care of the a.m. CT scans. Myra had provided Becky the wrong information. What's worse, Myra was one of the nurses in the boss's office complaining about Becky.

For the victims of ViperNurse, the problem isn't just that the bully is two-faced; the problem is that this nurse slowly influences others on the unit into negative thinking about his or her targets. ViperNurses rely on building trusting relationships and making their victims feel secure. A victim may reveal a weakness (e.g., a fear of talking to doctors) and then find out later that the entire department knows about it. The ViperNurse denies saying anything and is hurt that the victim would even think such a thing!

This nurse cannot be trusted. If you tell a ViperNurse something in confidence, it will leak out when the time is right for him or her. ViperNurse loves pitting people against each other for personal gain while denying any involvement. "Who? Little ole me?"

COVERT BEHAVIORS OF VIPERNURSE

While the covert behaviors of ViperNurse are more difficult to detect than those of her overt colleagues, there are some warning signs. ViperNurses tend to act like they are your best friend, go out of their way to help you, and may even share sensitive, personal information with you. Over time, you open up to ViperNurse and may feel compelled to share sensitive information with him or her.

Amanda was going through a rough time with her husband and began to share information with some of the older, more experienced nurses. They were so nice, always asking her how things were going and encouraging her to share her problems. It wasn't until Amanda got called into her boss's office and was told to focus on patients and not personal issues while at work that Amanda got the sense that several nurses didn't really have her best interests at heart. Then one of the nursing assistants pulled her aside and said, "Be careful who you say things to around here. The people who you think are your friends aren't." Amanda soon found out the experienced nurses she confided in were talking about her behind her back and telling the boss she was spending all night on the phone arguing with her husband. Amanda had been "zinged."

ViperNurses undermine, sabotage, and find ways to bully you without being obvious about it.

SORORITYNURSE (COVERT)

SororityNurse uses exclusion as his or her primary mode of operation. You're either in or you're out. If you're the new nurse, the standard is made clear to you very early in your orientation. "Be nice and obey us or we'll make your life miserable here." SororityNurse can bully without words but with powerful non-verbal signals such as crossing arms, giving the "death stare," turning his or her back to you, and walking away while you're speaking. SororityNurse shows favoritism and only helps the nurses who are "in."

SororityNurse may use tactics similar to those of ViperNurse but takes things to the next level. SororityNurse not only uses covert tactics to "zing" targets, but this nurse gathers a "posse" of nurses against the target. He or she orchestrates the group of "in" nurses to exclude anyone on the outside. For victims, being the target of consistent covert exclusion is easily as painful as being the target of overt behaviors such as yelling and humiliation.

At first, Julie was invited to lunch breaks, work activities, and social functions, but over time she noticed the nurses were ordering out for lunch without asking her if she wanted anything. They were planning happy hours but not inviting her. The unit nurses even started making excuses why they couldn't watch Julie's patients while she took a break. Julie was excluded.

Julie wasn't in the sorority because of the consistent, covert actions of SororityNurse. Other nurses on Julie's unit weren't necessarily intentional bullies; they had simply been poisoned against Julie by SororityNurse's tactics. Julie was left wondering what she did wrong.

On units where a number of nurses speak a native language different from the others, SororityNurse may use language to create barriers and exclude others. SororityNurse may encourage members of the "in" group to communicate using their native language in front of their targets. All it takes is for one of those in the sorority to glance at the target for that person to think the group is talking behind his or her back. Add a laugh or a roll of the eyes, and the target immediately thinks the group is making fun of him or her. SororityNurse knows this and uses this covert tactic to make her targets feel excluded.

> *Group conformity scares the pants off me because it's so often a prelude to cruelty towards anyone who doesn't want to—or can't—join the Big Parade.*
>
> ~ Bette Midler

COVERT BEHAVIORS OF SORORITYNURSE

SororityNurse uses exclusion, refusal to help, and sarcasm as his or her primary weapons. This bully is easier to spot than ViperNurse but is no less damaging to victims. SororityNurse sees to it that the group only celebrates birthdays of the nurses in their sorority, recognizes the accomplishments of their own, eats lunch together, covers each other's patients, and also protects each other. SororityNurse selects who's in and who's out.

Some nurses new to a unit recognize the sorority and decide to join as a way of fitting in and avoiding being bullied. This is a tempting solution, but sorority membership is never truly secure and safe. It's easy to get kicked out of the sorority if you lose the favor of SororityNurse. What's worse, a nurse who goes along with the sorority to fit in will likely find he or she is expected to participate in bullying those nurses who are excluded from the group.

BITTERNURSE (OVERT AND COVERT)

BitterNurse is green with envy. This bully downplays everyone else's accomplishments, never recognizes anyone's success, and thinks awards are just stupid. Anytime BitterNurse is asked to do something, this nurse wants to know what he or she will get out of it. "Why should I help you with your lecture? What's in it for me?" BitterNurse is hell-bent on not letting anyone get anything over on him or her, not even patients.

BitterNurse is different than EnergyVampire because this bully's focus is on downplaying accomplishments rather than broadly deflating energy. BitterNurse may be pleasant in every other way, but tell a "bitter nurse" that you got an award and look out!

BitterNurse frequently has to "one-up" each conversation, always having a last word or a more remarkable story than everyone else's. You may be describing how you did CPR on somebody at church on Sunday while BitterNurse chimes in to say, "That's nothing. I did CPR on three people at the same time during a hurricane!" Although BitterNurse may brag a bit like SuperNurse, this bully's primary mode of operation is to negate *your* accomplishments, not necessarily to promote his or hers.

Barb worked as a nurse recruiter in a large hospital. Although she loved her job, she wanted to advance her career. An executive position opened up for a nurse with experience in hiring and developing new nurses. Barb was excited and felt the job was the perfect fit for her. When she told her colleagues about it, most of them were enthusiastic and encouraged Barb to apply. However, Barb's friend and colleague, a classic BitterNurse, could only think about what it would mean for her if Barb left. Barb's "friend" was upset at the prospect. Not only did she discourage Barb from applying but went behind Barb's back and told Barb's boss to do everything she could to stop the promotion. With BitterNurse as a friend, Barb didn't need enemies!

> *I don't mean to sound bitter, cold, or cruel, but I am, so that's how it comes out.*
>
> ~ Bill Hicks

OVERT AND COVERT BEHAVIORS OF BITTERNURSE

Sometimes BitterNurse will actually challenge your accomplishments in front of others, going so far as to make light of or fun of them. BitterNurse may openly criticize and try to humiliate you if you receive any awards or accolades. "You got your BSN? Heck, that doesn't mean anything. It was a waste of time and money."

On the other hand, you might find out from others that BitterNurse expressed disdain at your achievement in a more subtle way. BitterNurse finds every opportunity to downplay the accomplishments of others, either overtly or covertly.

Chances are you have met one or more of the five classic types of bullies described in this chapter in your work environment. Of course, no one is a pure "type," and some of the behaviors overlap. It is the ability to recognize the behaviors, both overt and covert, that will allow you to respond to a bully attack effectively, no matter what the bully profile.

Bullies and other oppressors, as you can see from this chapter, adopt different roles. Scholars delve into the reasons behind these roles. For our purposes, it's enough to understand that an undercurrent of perceived power exists among oppressors. This, in conjunction with other factors, drives the different manifestations of bullying behavior.

Now that you can profile a bully and clearly identify overt and covert behaviors, it's time to turn your attention to a systematic process to launch a counter-attack. If you want to stop bully behavior directed at you, keep reading!

Chapter 7

Steps to Stop the Bullying

> *Often the right path is the one that may be hardest for you to follow. But the hard path is also the one that will make you grow as a human being.*
>
> ~ Karen Mueller Coombs

Whether you face overt or covert bullying behavior, it's time to demand the dignity every person deserves and end the silence and isolation that so often surrounds victims of bullying. As I mentioned in previous chapters, it takes moral courage to do the right thing, to speak up when you see wrongdoing to yourself and others, especially when you feel bruised and battered.

It may feel that it takes everything you have to speak up in the face of bullying, but the results will be worth the effort. Although you cannot control other people, you can learn to establish boundaries and minimize the impact others have on you, especially in the work environment. While you can't change entire systems, you can take action that decreases the likelihood of being a target and decreases the power of the bully on your unit.

Remind yourself that you deserve to work in an environment that is nurturing, supportive, and professional. You've worked hard to get your nursing degree. Make the commitment to yourself that you will not let anyone push you out of your right to practice nursing! This commitment is the first step to increasing patient safety, strengthening relationships, and creating a healthier work environment for yourself and others. Take a deep breath and believe you are doing the right thing.

> *"Nobody can make you feel inferior without your consent."*
>
> ~ Eleanor Roosevelt

STEPS TO STOP THE BULLYING

In this chapter, you'll discover strategies and steps to stop the bullying. Some of the strategies will work in the face of both overt and covert bullying. Others will be specific to one type or the other. Some strategies will make sense to you instantly while others may initially seem impossible. I suggest you read the entire chapter for understanding and then return with your own situations in mind. You CAN successfully take actions to reduce your attractiveness as a bully target. The secret, as in most difficult endeavors, is to summon your moral courage and take one step at a time.

If you find yourself the target of a bully, either overt or covert, follow these four general steps:

Step 1: Recognize you are a victim

Step 2: Mentally separate yourself from the bully

Step 3: Speak up

Step 4: Confront the bully

Note: Reading Step 4 may initiate a surge of hydrochloric acid in your stomach! The idea of confronting a bully may seem daunting, even impossible, but it can be done. The secret is to confront the behavior, not the person. For example, rather than confront a bully with "You always treat me with disrespect," you'll say "In this conversation so far, you've interrupted me three times. Please let me finish talking before you respond."

As you learn to name individual behaviors as inappropriate, you'll drain the bully's arsenal of weapons, one by one. As in any skill you are learning, success will come by taking small steps over time. With practice, you WILL succeed. Just remember to start small and be patient with yourself. Here are some important qualifiers:

- You don't have to begin practicing these steps with a queen bully! Start small and build your skills and your confidence.

- You can begin the step "speak up" by telling anyone you trust about the experiences you are having with a bully. Breaking the silence with a trusted friend outside of work is a good start.

- Confronting a bully doesn't mean you attempt to turn the tides and be someone you are not. In this case, confrontation means presenting facts in a calm and matter-of-fact way rather than trying to intimidate the intimidator! In fact, in the case of bullying, fighting fire with fire is both ineffective and inadvisable.

> *The way to develop self-confidence is to do the thing you fear and get a record of successful experiences behind you.*
>
> *~ William Jennings Bryan*

Step 1: Recognize You Are a Victim

Not all nurses have heard of the phrase "horizontal violence"; however, virtually every nurse knows the phrase, "Nurses eat their young." We all know the behavior although we may call it by different names. Some nurses, however, accept that bullying is an integral part of a tough profession, a necessary evil or an unfortunate reality. These nurses work to "toughen up" and seek strategies to survive on the job, at great personal expense. Nurses get desensitized or numb to the continuous attacks, to the point where bullying behavior appears normal to them.

The situation is similar to that of battered women being victimized by their spouses. Over time, they come to see the abusive behavior as their "normal." The situation is also similar to the classic "boiled frog" science experiment in which a frog failed to make an easy escape from a pot of boiling water because the condition of the water reached the boiling temperature gradually. The frog grew accustomed to the gradual change and did nothing to escape until it died.

Here's an extreme example: June had been married to Frank for 48 years. Although she complained about Frank to her kids and now grandkids, she did nothing to stop his verbal attacks on her. She was silent while in his presence. Once, June's granddaughter was traveling in the car with the couple and witnessed an onslaught of criticism and put-downs from her grandfather. After the trip (away from Frank's view), the granddaughter hugged June and told her how sorry she felt for her because of the way Grandpa was treating her.

June, surprised, replied, "Oh. I didn't think Grandpa was being that mean. That's just the way he always talks to me." June had lost the ability to recognize her husband's behaviors as bullying and abusive.

The first step on the journey to stop bullying is to recognize you're being victimized. As I've mentioned before, many nurses think that being bullied is a rite of passage, something that all nurses must go through to be accepted in the workplace. Therefore, when they find themselves yelled at, given the worst assignments over and over, or unsupported, they think this is normal behavior.

Make no mistake about it: if you have been on the receiving end of this type of behavior delivered by the same nurses over a period of time, you are the victim of one or more bullies. The key is to recognize it as bullying, as destructive, and as behavior that doesn't belong in the nursing profession. You deserve to work in an environment that is nurturing and supportive. Period!

Action Step

If you think you might be a victim, spend the next week or so observing how your co-workers behave. Compare their behaviors to the overt and covert characteristics listed in Chapter 2. Do you see these behaviors in your colleagues? Are they directed at you? Are they directed at others? Have you grown so accustomed to bully behavior on your unit that you've come to think of it as normal?

STEP 2: MENTALLY SEPARATE YOURSELF FROM THE BULLY

As we discussed in Chapter 3, if you are the victim of a bully, it's not your fault. The problem lies with the bully, not you. Many times when yelled at or made to feel stupid, victims turn inward and blame themselves. "What did I do to make him or her mad? I should have known that. I'm so stupid." If you find yourself going down this mental path, stop and recognize that although you may make mistakes, being degraded for them isn't acceptable.

Separating from the bully's behavior can be the most powerful, liberating step you can take to protect yourself from the toxic impact of the bully. Think back to the times when you were yelled at, criticized, or not supported by your co-workers. Think about a time you suspected that although someone was nice to you, he or she might be secretly stabbing you in the back. How did you feel in these instances? Did you feel embarrassed, humiliated, or anxious?

Now, pretend you are simply an observer watching the events you've recalled unfold. Can you see how the problem is with the bully and not with you? Even if you did make a mistake, it's unprofessional and inappropriate for another person to yell, openly criticize, or "zing" you when you're not looking. You don't deserve to be berated or publicly humiliated for a mistake. No one does.

Try catching yourself going down a path of self-blame and redirect your thoughts. Let's say SuperNurse is at it again. She walks into the nurses' station and says in a loud, condescending voice, "Who is the idiot that left the medcart open in the hallway near room 22?"

You immediately get a knot in your stomach because you know it's you. You got called out to the desk by the secretary and just forgot to go back and shut and lock your medcart. However, SuperNurse isn't letting it go. You can hear her shouting, "Who's the idiot? Come on. I know it's one of you baby nurses."

In the moments that SuperNurse is openly criticizing, pause and think. Is he or she handling this situation as a professional? Is this appropriate behavior to yell in the middle of the nurses' station where everyone can hear: visitors, ancillary staff, patients, etc.? Once you recognize that SuperNurse's behavior is inappropriate, mentally separate yourself and your mistake from his or her response. You made a mistake by leaving your medcart open. But that doesn't justify the inappropriate behavior. Separate, then acknowledge that it's your medcart, get up and lock it. Avoid getting into a confrontation with SuperNurse at this point.

The key is to separate yourself from the bully and realize that he or she is the one with the problem, not you. Emotionally detaching yourself from the bully's behavior will defuse much of your anxiety and help you to move forward productively.

Action Step

When you are on the receiving end of a bully's overt or covert behavior and start blaming yourself or feeling bad, catch yourself. Try picturing a mental stop sign as a symbol that you are going down a path of self-blame. Take a mental step back and look at the situation objectively, through an observer's eyes. Can you separate yourself from the bully?

Step 3: Speak Up

Many nurses, especially new ones, are victimized at work yet don't say a word. Perhaps it's because they're embarrassed, don't think anyone can help, are afraid of retaliation, or don't know who to turn to. Over time, victims can suffer emotional and physical consequences to the point where they quit without anyone knowing what they were going through. The key is to speak up. Don't suffer in silence. Let somebody know you're experiencing inappropriate behavior by your co-workers.

Talking to your preceptor, nurse educator, a colleague, or even a friend about your situation is an important step to breaking the cycle. If you have been suffering in silence, choose the safest, most supportive person you know to talk to. Even if you speak to a person who is outside of your work unit and unfamiliar with nursing, you will have taken an important first step.

Courtney started her career as a new nurse on a busy cardiac unit. At first, she was excited to work with the other nurses, physicians, and to finally provide care to her patients as a Registered Nurse and not "just a student." Very quickly, however, Courtney realized she was working in a toxic unit plagued with overt bullies. She was yelled at, left on her own while the other nurses sat around at the nurses' station gossiping, and frequently criticized for not knowing everything. Courtney began to feel physically ill before each shift as she dreaded coming to work. Courtney considered quitting.

Three months into her new job, Courtney attended an in-service facilitated by an educator she had met during her orientation. During a break, the educator approached Courtney and asked her how things were going. Courtney burst into tears. Courtney shared her bullying stories with the educator and explained that she was tempted to quit. The educator listened to Courtney and convinced her not to quit, and not to allow the bullies to destroy her dreams. The educator became a mentor for Courtney and helped her develop the skill and the moral courage she needed to confront the bullies. By speaking up, Courtney was able to make the invisible—visible. Her mentor helped Courtney to recognize the bullying behavior, mentally separate herself from their attacks, and address specific overt and covert behaviors.

Courtney has been happily working on the same unit for the last three years. Although some of the bullies are still present, Courtney has acquired the skills necessary to set boundaries and stop the bully attacks. She loves her work and is grateful she spoke up.

If you are working in a toxic environment, speak up. Find somebody that you can share your experiences with who might be able to help you cope. Speaking up requires moral courage. Pause, take a deep breath, and know you are making the right decision.

If there isn't anyone in your organization you feel comfortable speaking to, find an external support person. Social media sites, such as LinkedIn.com, are great resources for nurses to post questions, ask for advice, and share experiences. The key is to talk to somebody who is supportive, who will listen, and who will help.

Action Step

Make a list of the people you feel comfortable sharing your experiences with. Set up some time to talk with one of them. At first, this might be someone you trust that doesn't work with you. Just make a commitment to speak up.

STEP 4: CONFRONT THE BULLY

Once you've strengthened your moral courage muscle by recognizing, mentally separating, and speaking up, it's time to plan your strategy to confront.

Note: This step requires more moral courage than any other. While speaking up takes a certain amount of courage, actually confronting a bully takes even more. Because of this, it is imperative that you plan your confrontation.

As we have seen in Chapter 2, most bully activity can be identified as either overt or covert. Start by identifying the behavior as overt or covert and then plan the appropriate strategy that will give you the greatest chance to counter. We'll begin with one strategy that works for both overt and covert behavior: *naming the behavior.*

> *Our lives begin to end the day we become silent about things that matter.*
> ~ Martin Luther King Jr.

NAMING THE BEHAVIOR

The single most powerful response you can make in the face of either overt or covert bully behavior is to name it. Calling the bully on his or her behavior as it occurs can stop things immediately and prevent an escalation of that behavior.

Bullies who feel a sense of power during their overt tirades gain momentum as they scream and yell. Interrupting a bully midstream and labeling the behavior can act as a defibrillator, short-circuiting the verbal assault.

Likewise, when you work with a colleague who is secretly trying to sabotage you, rolling his or her eyes behind your back, or undermining your ability, acknowledging that you are aware of the behavior brings the bully out of the closet. The bully may think his or her efforts are going unnoticed until you name it. Typically once the covert bully's cover is gone, the behavior stops.

> *A lot of people are afraid to tell the truth, to say no.*
> *That's where toughness comes into play. Toughness is*
> *not being a bully. It's having backbone.*
>   ~ Robert Kiyosaki

EXAMPLES OF NAMING THE BEHAVIOR

Keep in mind, naming the behavior utilizes assertive communication skills. Naming it uses open and honest communication as in assertive communication, but it also describes the behavior of the bully. To be effective, naming the behavior must describe specific, observable actions.

If a target says to a bully, "You always give me the worst assignments," the bully can deny the charge. If the target says, "For three shifts in a row, I've had one more patient than the other nurses on my shift," it's hard for the bully to deny this fact. Any attempt to name bullying behavior must include observable, verifiable facts and/or behavior.

Using the previous example with SuperNurse yelling about the unlocked medcart, you could say, "I left the medcart open. Yelling and referring to your co-worker as an idiot in front of patients and their families is inappropriate."

Here are some additional examples of naming both covert and overt behavior. The specific, observable behaviors are in bold print.

- "You are **yelling and screaming** (overt) at me in front of patients and their families."

- "I saw you **roll your eyes** (overt) when I asked you for help with a patient."

- "This morning during the staff meeting, when our manager acknowledged my recent BSN achievement, **I heard you snicker** and **saw you roll your eyes** (overt)."

- "I'll be willing to talk about my mistake when you are ready to speak privately **rather than calling me a baby in the middle of the unit** (overt)."

- "You told me to go home and not to complete my work. However, nurses on the unit told me you were **complaining about me** throughout the night. I would appreciate if you would give me direct feedback instead of **talking about me behind my back** (covert)."

Naming the Behavior—Overt

When Risa started working on a neurosurgical step-down unit, she wasn't new to nursing. However, she was new to neuroscience nursing. She felt like a new nurse all over again. Initially, Risa was apprehensive, knowing she would be working with brain surgeons who were notorious for yelling and making unrealistic demands on the nursing staff. Risa's preceptor warned her about a particular neurosurgeon who had a habit of yelling at any nurse who didn't get his patients out of bed by 6 a.m. each morning.

One early morning after a crazy night, Risa didn't get her patient in the chair before the neurosurgeon rounded. While in another patient's room, Risa heard the neurosurgeon yell for her in the hallway. She felt a knot forming in her stomach but walked into the hallway and acknowledged the neurosurgeon. "Why isn't my patient out of bed?" the neurosurgeon screamed.

Somehow, through the yelling and screaming, Risa had a moment of clarity and recognized the neurosurgeon's behavior was inappropriate. Risa was then able to mentally separate herself from the situation. She couldn't believe that she and her colleagues all cowered to this surgeon and his tirades. In that moment, Risa was no longer willing to let the surgeon yell and scream at her; after all, she knew the importance of getting patients out of bed. A crisis situation with another patient had delayed her that particular morning.

Risa stood a little taller, looked the neurosurgeon in the eye and said, "You are yelling and screaming in the middle of the hallway where patients can hear. You haven't even tried to find out if there is a reason your patient isn't out of bed yet." Risa said this in a calm, professional manner, looking at the surgeon right in the eye.

The physician actually stepped back a bit and stopped yelling. Perhaps he was surprised by Risa's comment and the fact that she didn't make excuses. He answered in a much softer voice, "I'm not yelling at you. I'm just angry that you didn't get my patient out of bed."

Risa replied, "Well, I could hear your voice all the way at the end of the hallway and I'm sure the patients could hear you too." The surgeon then apologized for yelling and asked Risa why she hadn't gotten the patient in the chair yet. As Risa explained, the doctor even walked into the patient's room with Risa and helped her get the patient out of bed. Anytime the surgeon started his yelling on the unit after that, Risa would interrupt him with a "you're yelling" warning and he would adjust his volume.

NAMING THE BEHAVIOR—COVERT BEHAVIOR

Christine was a new educator working in staff development. She was young, energetic and full of innovative and fun teaching methods. Marsha, the director of education, had hired her.

Marsha was older, well respected, and usually received a lot of attention for her ability to captivate an audience, at least until Christine arrived. Within a matter of months, Marsha was getting inundated with praises and compliments regarding Christine. The Chief Nursing Officer even recommended that Christine lead the monthly nursing forums instead of Marsha.

Over the course of the next few months, Christine noticed that Marsha "forgot" to invite her to meetings, and she mysteriously left her out of a few after-work activities. Then Christine began to find herself in situations in which Marsha would have to come in and "save the day." Over time, Christine started to recognize that Marsha was sabotaging her career by deliberately putting her in situations where she looked bad.

Christine asked to meet with Marsha to discuss this issue. She started the conversation by saying that it was important for her to have a trusting relationship with Marsha. She then told her that she felt Marsha was sabotaging her career and provided her with objective examples she had been gathering over time. Marsha was definitely caught off guard and although she denied her behavior, she stopped the covert sabotaging. Christine stayed in the department for three years until her efforts got her a promotion in another organization.

Action Step

For the next few weeks, observe your co-workers' behaviors. Identify behaviors you observe as overt or covert. Write down how you would "name" that behavior. It's okay to name positive behavior (and express appreciation) as well as bad behavior. Open, honest communication includes both!

WALK AWAY FROM OVERT BULLYING

Another effective strategy for overt behavior is simply to walk away. Some bullies, especially SuperNurses, love an audience. Similar to actors in a theatrical performance, these bullies need an audience for the performance to continue. If you walk away, you take the audience away with you. Seldom will a bully continue screaming, yelling, or criticizing somebody without an audience.

Here are some sample situations and possible responses that involve walking away from overt bully behavior:

- YELLING AND SCREAMING
  Interrupt the bully in the midst of the yelling and say, "I'll be willing to continue the conversation when you are able to do so without yelling." If the yelling doesn't stop, turn around and walk away.

- OPENLY CRITICIZING
  Interrupt the bully and say, "I am receptive to feedback. However, if you can't deliver that feedback calmly and respectfully, I am not willing to listen." If the bully gets defensive and continues to criticize, turn around and walk away.

- OPENLY MINIMIZING YOUR ACCOMPLISHMENTS
  "I respect the decisions you've made regarding education and I expect you to respect mine." If the bully continues, turn around and walk away.

It takes moral courage to walk away from a bully who's yelling or openly criticizing you, but it's a powerful defensive tactic.

Action Step

Make a list of potential situations where you may find yourself under a bully's attack. Write down how you would respond. As you might rehearse in the theater, practice saying your lines and walking away.

SUPPORT YOUR CONVERSATION WITH FACTS AND DOCUMENTATION

It's much harder for a covert bully to continue a stealth attack if you consistently bring up the truth. Like Mr. Spock in *Star Trek*, giving the facts in a non-emotional manner shows the bully you're aware of his or her bullying behaviors. The power in this is that it lets everyone else know too. When you speak the truth, you take control. The most effective way to speak the truth is to document facts and present them in a matter-of-fact statement.

For example, Liz dreaded when Robin was in charge because Liz knew she would get the worst assignments. Once Liz recognized the pattern as bullying, she started documenting her assignments versus those of her colleagues. Over a period of three weeks, Liz had enough documentation to show Robin was unfair to her.

Liz came to work early one day, asked to speak with Robin before she made the assignments, and presented her findings in a calm and factual way. "Robin, help me to understand why when you're in charge, I consistently get the isolation, post-op and detox patients."

Robin initially defended herself, telling Liz that she was just being sensitive. Liz then presented a log of her assignments compared to the other nurses. It was clear to Robin that Liz was serious and she stopped the unfair assignments.

Confronting a bully isn't easy and it doesn't always work. However, failure to confront never works! Confronting a bully requires assertiveness and the moral courage to reach beyond your comfort zone.

Action Step

Write your signature on a piece of paper. Now, switch hands and write your signature with your non-dominant hand. Difficult, right?

Although uncomfortable, awkward and challenging, you can write with your non-dominant hand. With practice and time, your signature written with your non-dominant hand may look similar to the one written with your dominant hand.

Confronting bullying behavior isn't easy but you can do it. Just like practicing your signature with your non-dominant hand, it may feel awkward and uncomfortable, but with practice and a dose of moral courage, you can do it.

The steps described in this chapter are all effective in addressing many bully situations. Separating yourself from the situation, speaking up, naming the behavior, walking away, and documenting facts are powerful anti-bully tactics, especially if you use these tactics consistently.

There are situations, however, where bully behavior is entrenched and supported by a unit or organization's culture. When this is the case, formal action is needed. Chapter 8 provides details of formal action and what to do if even that doesn't work. Chapter 8 also describes steps that witnesses of bully attacks can take to effectively intervene.

> *The truth is incontrovertible; malice may attack it, ignorance my deride it, but in the end, there it is.*
> ~ Winston Churchill

Chapter 8

When Enough Is Enough

You now know the steps to reducing or eliminating bully attacks: recognize, separate, speak up, and confront. What if you've gone through the steps and the bullying behavior continues? What if the bullying actually gets worse as your particular bully thrives on knowing his or her victims are aware? What if the bully launches a retaliation attack? If you find yourself in one of these situations, it's time to take things to the next organizational level. You've worked hard to get your nursing degree and you need to protect your career.

Make a Formal Written Complaint

Making a complaint is different from complaining. Complaining may be viewed as venting, whining, or even gossiping. Making a formal complaint is delivering an official assertive statement that a situation is inappropriate and unacceptable. It tells the recipient you are serious and expect an official response.

Start with a documentation record of the bully's behavior(s). If impartial witnesses were present, include their names. This record needs to be written objectively and include dates, times, and an accurate description of the behavior. Once you have sufficient documentation, make an appointment with your manager or human resource (HR) representative.

Always start with your manager, unless your manager is the bully; your manager is good friends with the bully and you don't trust his or her intent; or you've already approached your manager with objective information.

Do you see the difference between complaining and making a formal complaint? Bursting into your manager's office or HR department venting about bad behavior isn't taken as seriously as making an appointment and handing your manager or the HR representative a detailed written account of the bullying behavior. When you lodge a formal complaint, your manager or HR representative has no choice but to take your complaint seriously.

By law, every organization is expected to establish a code of conduct and is held accountable not only to establish a zero tolerance for bullying, but to also follow through on formal complaints. If a manager ignores a formal complaint, the organization could be held liable for violating regulations regarding a hostile work environment.

Obviously, you can't control the culture of your organization and/or how thoroughly officials investigate complaints and take action against bullying behavior. You do, however, owe it to yourself to make a formal complaint when all else has failed. If nothing changes as a result of your complaint, you may have "earned" the right to leave and pursue a position in a less toxic environment.

You Can Earn Your Right to Leave

Peggy left her husband after decades of marriage. Her daughters were teenagers at the time and for several years, Peggy blamed herself for every bad decision her daughters made and every bad relationship they had, thinking that if she hadn't left, their lives would have been better. Peggy was consumed with guilt. Then Peggy read an advice column in a magazine and realized she had earned the right to leave.

Peggy had done everything she could to keep the marriage healthy: counseling, compromising, sacrificing, pleading for her husband to change, and, even for a while, accepting being unhappy just to keep the family together. Nothing worked until she chose to leave. Once Peggy realized she had done everything she could, she stopped blaming herself, let go of the guilt, and started looking forward to a brighter future.

The advice Peggy found can apply to nursing too. You earn your right to leave by doing everything you can to make the bullying stop—no matter how difficult. If you can honestly look back and say you've done your part and nothing significantly changed, you have the right to leave with a clean conscience and head held high. The problem is with the organization, not with you.

Don't stay in an abusive environment thinking it will get better. It seldom does. You deserve to work in an environment that is supportive, nurturing, and professional.

WHEN YOU ARE THE WITNESS TO BULLY ATTACKS

An international workplace nursing survey reported 80% of respondents witnessed a nursing colleague subjected to horizontal violence. Fifty-one percent of the perpetrators in these cases were other nurses. To end bullying requires everyone to act when they witness other nurses subjected to bullying behavior.

Here are steps you can take when you are witness to bully behavior, especially behavior that repeats over time:

Step 1: Recognize

Step 2: Intervene

Step 3: Document

Step 4: Support

> *Now I say that with cruelty and oppression it is everybody's business to interfere when they see it.*
> ~ Anna Sewell

Step 1: Recognize

The first step is to recognize bullying for what it is—inappropriate and toxic behavior with impact that extends far beyond the victim. Bully behavior is dangerous to victims, their colleagues, the culture of a unit, and patients. Bully behavior is not a necessary evil in a tough profession, and it is not behavior that should be tolerated in some nurses.

Studies show the most powerful action in eliminating bullying is for the witness to take action and intervene on behalf of the victim. If you witness bullying behavior, you owe it to your colleagues, your patients, and your profession to respond. A beginning step is to name the behavior as you see it.

Here are some situations you might witness:

- BEHAVIOR
  You overhear an experienced nurse refer to a new nurse as a "baby nurse."

- YOUR RESPONSE

  "Yes. She is a new nurse and we need to do everything we can to help her succeed. Referring to her as a "baby nurse" is neither respectful nor helpful."

- BEHAVIOR

  The charge nurse is making assignments. You over-hear her say she is giving "the train wreck" to the agency nurse who is new to the unit.

- YOUR RESPONSE

  "If you were the challenging patient, would you want a nurse who has never worked on this unit to care for you? What's best for the patient? Please change the agency nurse's assignment to an easier one."

STEP 2: INTERVENE

We all witness unprofessional behavior but don't always intervene. It takes a great deal of moral courage to interrupt a bully who is yelling at someone or stand up to a bully you know is sabotaging a co-worker. Moral courage takes deliberate thought and a willingness to be uncomfortable confronting someone you know is disruptive, especially if you fear retaliation. However, when you are faced with the decision to intervene or not to intervene, pause, take a deep breath, flex your moral courage muscles, and do the right thing.

STEP 3: DOCUMENT

If naming the behavior doesn't work and the bullying contin-ues, formally report the problem to your manager or a repre-sentative from the HR department, or both. To prepare, keep a log of specific behaviors you witness on specific dates. The more specific and verifiable your documentation, the more likely you are to get a positive result. If you've shared information and documentation about one or more incidents, and nothing changes, consider filing a formal complaint.

STEP 4: SUPPORT

Finally, offer support to a victim of bullying by letting that person know you consider any bully behavior unacceptable. Offer honest words of encouragement regarding the victim's skills as a nurse. Help the person regroup and refocus on patient care. Offering support to a victim may prevent a nurse from quitting his or her job or the nursing profession.

WHEN YOU ARE THE MANAGER

The manager of a department sets the tone for behavior, performance, and accountability. He or she holds the quintessential role in an organization's ability to combat bullying. Unfortunately, managers are often not equipped with the skills necessary to deal with bullying.

Managers are typically promoted from the ranks of nurses and may have become conditioned to accept bullying as part of a tough profession. To make matters worse, managers who do seek to stop bullying are often not supported in their intent to follow through on discipline.

Judy was a new unit manager on a large medical surgical unit. During her first week, several employees warned her about Sylvia and Martha, a.k.a., "the bullies." Within a few weeks, Judy was witness not only to bad behavior but bad and potentially unsafe practice. When she asked for support from the HR department, Judy faced a litany of red tape that prevented her from formally disciplining Sylvia and Martha.

Judy was frequently told that she had to have multiple witnesses, signed documents from co-workers, and other vestiges of "red tape." One night, a nurse complaining that Sylvia had walked off the unit while her patient was experiencing a rapid heart rhythm paged Judy at 3 a.m. Sylvia was overheard saying, "Well, he'll have to wait until I get back from my smoke break." Luckily, Sylvia's co-workers responded and took care of the patient.

It took Judy a lot of time and effort, but she terminated both Sylvia and Martha, based on their performance, including bad and unsafe behavior. This significantly reduced the stress on the entire unit. Because of the red tape, however, the effort required Judy to summon her moral courage on behalf of her employees and her patients. Everyone benefited when two toxic nurses were no longer on the unit.

If you are a manager, it is your responsibility to create and maintain a healthy working environment for your employees. Even if you manage a unit plagued with bullies, by incorporating the following strategies, you can turn things around:

- Set expectations
- Determine consequences for violating expectations
- Follow through on consequences

> *With realization of one's own potential and self-confidence in one's ability, one can build a better world.*
> ~ Dalai Lama

SET EXPECTATIONS

Take a moment to envision the ideal work environment where bullying doesn't exist, nurses treat each other with respect, and all employees go out of their way to support each other. What does it look like? What outcomes can you see as a result?

Now, create a goal that encompasses your vision of the ideal work environment. The most effective goals are tangible and objective as well as defined by measurable behaviors.

- VAGUE GOAL
  Everybody needs to get along.

- BETTER GOAL
  Employees will demonstrate respect and support towards each other, patients, patient families, and other members of the healthcare team.

Once you establish this expectation, get your nursing staff involved in defining the objective behaviors that represent the goal. Nurses, like all professionals, want to be autonomous and involved in decision-making. When nurses believe they have a say in how the unit runs, they will be more invested in the process.

Guide your team to answer the question: What does "demonstrate respect" mean? Perhaps it's smiling, always telling somebody your name, greeting visitors, welcoming new employees in a particular way, etc.

What does "support" mean? Perhaps it's answering call lights even if the patient calling isn't yours, giving the new nurse a lighter assignment when he or she is off orientation, always putting patient needs first, and pitching in to help when a nurse has a heavier assignment, etc.

Equally important is to define the behaviors that *do not* represent respect and support, such as cursing, criticizing in front of others, ignoring a call light from a patient that isn't yours, etc.

By getting the employees to identify the behaviors you want and the behaviors you don't want, you increase their intrinsic motivation to maintain and enforce the goal. You determine the goal; let your employees determine the process of getting there.

When all employees can articulate the expected goals and behaviors, you can hold them accountable.

IDENTIFY CONSEQUENCES

Once you've identified the goal and behaviors, the next step is to identify consequences for employees who violate expectations. Your employees can also suggest consequences but might need guidance from you, especially as they might not be knowledgeable about the disciplinary action process. Encourage your employees to take an active role in determining consequences.

Here are a few examples of expected behaviors with identified consequences:

- BEHAVIOR
  Answering call lights is the responsibility of all employees, independent of assignments.

  Employees will respond to all call lights within 30 seconds, either through the call system or by walking into the patient's room.

- CONSEQUENCE
  The consequence for ignoring a call light or if an employee is overhead saying, "That's not my patient," is disciplinary action. Disciplinary action includes the following:

  - First Offense: Verbal warning

- Second Offense: Written warning placed in employee's file

- Third Offense: The employee will not be permitted to participate in self-scheduling during the next schedule*

- Fourth Offense: Suspension

- Fifth Offense: Termination

*Note: The third offense consequence on this list might not be something a manager would think of as discipline. However, self-scheduling is highly valued by employees. If nurses lose the opportunity to participate in self-scheduling as a consequence, they will monitor their own behavior to avoid the consequence.

FOLLOW THROUGH ON CONSEQUENCES

The biggest complaint I hear from nurses is that managers don't hold their co-workers accountable. Sometimes employees are right. Many managers set expectations, identify consequences, and then fail to follow through. When employees are not held accountable, behaviors return to their previous state. Over time, morale drops and employees disengage.

Holding your employees accountable and following through on consequences can be difficult, especially if an employee generally demonstrates good performance, is your friend, or has problems at home. However, you must be consistent and hold everyone accountable to the same agreed-upon standards.

Jack was a nursing assistant known for outbursts of anger and foul language on the unit. When people complained to the unit manager about Jack, she always defended him, saying he had a rough life at home. Jack was working two jobs to support his parents and disabled sister.

The unit established expectations for behavior on the unit that included "no cursing." Everyone agreed, including Jack.

Two weeks later, several staff members overheard Jack yelling in the hallway and cursing as he walked into a patient's room. A nurse immediately addressed the issue with Jack and asked him to stop yelling and cursing. The nurse documented the incident, obtained signatures from witnesses, and presented the complaint to the manager. The manager's reply was that Jack had had a really bad day because he had to admit his sister to a skilled facility as he was unable to continue caring for her. The consequence for cursing wasn't enforced. Needless to say, both the commitment to the agreed-upon standards and morale suffered.

Patty never answered a patient's light unless it was her own. When the unit got together to set expectations for behavior, answering all call lights even if it's not your patient's was one of the agreed-upon expectations. The consequence for anyone who walked past a call light without answering it was scheduling last on the self-schedule for the next month.

Patty and the unit manager were good friends. They went to nursing school together, went out to social events, and frequently ate lunch together. Everyone waited for the moment when Patty would ignore a call light. How would the manager, Patty's friend, respond? And then the moment came.

Three people witnessed Patty ignoring a call light as she walked past saying, "That's not my patient." All three staff members documented the situation and presented it to the manager. Sure enough, as agreed, Patty's name was last on the list to schedule the next month. If the unit manager could "punish" her good friend, that meant she was holding everyone accountable. Morale rose and behaviors changed.

Disciplining your friend or someone who has extenuating life circumstances isn't easy. It requires moral courage to call your friend on his or her behavior and follow through on the consequences set forth by your staff. When facing a difficult conversation, here is a suggestion:

> Start the conversation by saying, "I need to have a conversation with you, but I'm uncomfortable having it. Our relationship is important to me and I don't want to jeopardize it." Then discuss the violation of behavior and deliver the consequence as you would to any employee. If the recipient gets defensive, remind him or her that as the manager, you need to maintain objectivity and consistency.

Note: Sometimes an employee is on the disciplinary path but because of confidentiality, the other employees might not be aware and inadvertently think nothing is being done. That employee might need just one more incident and will be terminated, but the other employees might think he or she is getting away with bad behavior.

BONUS TIP FOR MANAGERS: EMPOWER PEER-TO-PEER ACCOUNTABILITY

Encouraging peer-to-peer accountability can completely transform a unit and take unnecessary burdens off the manager. Peer-to-peer accountability involves giving feedback to a colleague using direct, assertive communication in an effort to address or clarify a behavior.

For example, imagine Katrina consistently arrives late for work, affecting Troy's ability to leave on time and catch his bus. In a unit that supports peer-to-peer accountability, Troy will have a direct conversation with Katrina about how her consistent late arrival affects Troy's ability to get home on time. This direct conversation will be Troy's first attempt to solve the problem, peer-to-peer. Only if Katrina continues to be late will Troy approach the department manager.

After a few weeks as new unit manager, Brittany dreaded arriving on her unit. Many mornings began with a line of employees outside the door to her office, waiting for her arrival. Most often, her employees wanted to complain about other employees.

At first, Brittany assumed she was responsible for handling every complaint and frequently found herself caught in the middle over employee squabbles. Things began to change when Brittany challenged her own assumption and response. She began to establish peer-to-peer accountability and teach her employees how to hold each other accountable. Over time, Brittany spent less time helping employees resolve their squabbles and more time actually managing her unit.

Action Step

Whether you are a manager or a co-worker, try the following response the next time a staff member complains to you about a colleague's behavior: "Have you shared this with him or her?"

Changing human behaviors is difficult at best. However, when the stars are in alignment, behaviors can change. It takes a manager who can set expectations and consistently hold employees accountable to address inappropriate behaviors—experienced or witnessed.

Whether you are the victim of a bully, a witness to bullying, or a manager, you need moral courage and persistence to address bad behavior. You owe it to yourself and to those on your unit to make the effort to stop the bullying. If you've followed the steps, done your best, and still nothing changes, however, you've earned the right to leave. Don't stay in a toxic environment without hope for improvement. Get out!

Leaving a persistently hostile environment makes sense, unless, of course, you discover that you are one of the contributors to that hostile environment. It's possible that as you have been reading this book, you have discovered bully behavior in yourself, whether that behavior is deliberate or inadvertent. If so, you don't have to beat yourself up or think of yourself as a bad person. Chapter 9 has important advice for you.

CHAPTER 9

WHAT TO DO IF THE BULLY IS YOU

> *I've failed over and over and over again in my life and that is why I succeed.*
>
> ~ Michael Jordan

If hundreds of thousands of nurses in the country are talking about the bullies, we have to ask ourselves, "Who are the bullies?" The answer is that we are. We are the bullies, or at least we have to consider that we might be. Perhaps we're not the queen bully, but maybe we've succumbed to bullying behaviors to fit in or be accepted into the social hierarchy of our working environments.

Susan was invited to a workshop to discuss horizontal violence. She had been a nurse for over 20 years and looked forward to sharing her insights. While her colleagues were sharing their experiences, mostly as victims, Susan kept quiet. Susan then stood up and said, "I used to be a bully." She proceeded to share her story and give the rest of the group a glimpse into the mind of a bully. Susan told the group that in her mind, she had been "getting the job done." This required her at times to give out quick, abrupt orders, make demands on others, and occasionally yell at her co-workers. In her mind, she had been just doing her job.

It wasn't until Susan overheard some of her co-workers referring to her as "Nurse Ratchet" and saying they felt sorry for any new nurses assigned to Susan as her orientee, that she realized her effect on other people. When Susan asked her boss if her co-workers ever complained about her, her boss put her head down and said, "All the time." When Susan asked why she hadn't told her about the problem, her boss said she had tried to several times but Susan just hadn't listened.

Why was Susan able to see her behavior through others' eyes that day but not before? Couldn't she see how her overt yelling and barking demands were characteristics of a bully? Susan said that although she knew she was abrasive, she justified her behaviors "for the good of the patient." For 20 years, Susan was known as a bully. It wasn't until she was able to self-reflect and see herself through the eyes of others that she changed her behavior.

How do you know if you're a bully? The first step is to be honest enough to consider your behaviors and ask if they mimic any of those we've discussed thus far. Take an introspective look at your behaviors to see if they contribute to horizontal violence in the workplace. It's a difficult thing to open yourself for scrutiny and awareness of your own behaviors, but such openness is a quality of both maturity and professionalism.

You may feel very uncomfortable turning the mirror on yourself. However, try to push through that discomfort and know that growing comes through discomfort.

Once, during a time when I was uncomfortable in a new job role and was feeling incompetent, a colleague said, "If you want to be a good tennis player, you have to play with people who are better than you, people who challenge you to grow. If you only play tennis with people as good as you, you will never feel the joy of new skills and accomplishment. It is through the discomfort that you grow."

Bully Behavior Assessment

Please answer the following questions by placing an "X" in the Yes or No box.

In my work environment . . .		Yes	No
1	I roll my eyes or make mean faces behind other people's backs		
2	I enjoy confrontations with people I know I can dominate		
3	I talk about other people in negative ways when they are not around		
4	I have purposely not invited somebody to a work party or event		
5	I have made fun of others because they are different		
6	I go out of my way to help some of my co-workers but not others		
7	If I'm in charge, I deliberately give the easier assignments to nurses I like		
8	I justify behaviors that help new nurses "toughen up"		
9	I sometimes ridicule a new or inexperienced co-worker		
10	Sometimes I make people cry at work		
11	Other people seem unreasonably upset by the things I say or do		
12	I think most of my co-workers are incompetent		
13	Other people seem scared to give me their opinions		

| 14 | New or inexperienced nurses rarely ask me for help more than once or twice | | |
| 15 | I've been told that I intimidate other people | | |

If you've answered "Yes" to more than three questions, you may be a bully. This may come as a shock, or you may already know that some of your behaviors are viewed as horizontal violence.

Of course, answering "Yes" to some of the questions doesn't mean you are a queen bully. There are degrees of bullying behavior. Whatever degree you find in yourself is the degree to which you need to change. Recognizing the need to change is usually the toughest part.

What if you recognize that you've adopted some of these behaviors as a way to fit in? Perhaps you didn't start out being a bully but took on the "if you can't beat them, join them" attitude to protect yourself. Does this mean that you are a bad person? Does it justify your behaviors?

You may have unintentionally joined the "sorority" as a way to avoid becoming the victim. You might be a nice person who has joined forces with the bullies gradually, without realizing you were engaging in the behaviors you were trying to avoid. Perhaps you can be viewed as an accidental bully.

Carly was nervous starting her first job as a nurse. The only unit with openings was a unit with a reputation for "nurses eating their young." Carly had realistic knowledge of the queen bully and her sorority because she had had a clinical rotation on that unit. Carly had witnessed how the bullies excluded some of the nurses, talked behind their backs, and deliberately sabotaged newer nurses. What should she do? How could she survive as a new nurse in a unit that "ate" new nurses? Carly's strategy? Become friends with the bullies and become one of their sorority sisters.

At first, Carly brought in goodies: cookies, candy, and doughnuts, making sure the bullies got first pick. Then Carly overtly praised sorority members, answered their call lights, helped them with their patients, and even offered to watch their patients while the "in" nurses took breaks. Shortly after Carly completed her orientation, she was part of the "in" group or sorority. She got the easier assignments, was invited to parties, and was included in after-work activities.

Carly quickly learned, however, that with the benefits of being "in" came certain expectations. Carly was expected to take part in the negative treatment of other nurses, those who weren't in the sorority. This meant that when Carly was in charge, she was expected to "dump" on the new nurses as well as any nurse the bullies identified as a target. She was expected to join in conversations bad-mouthing other nurses. If a nurse excluded from the group asked Carly for help with a patient or to cover during a break, Carly was expected to say, "No."

Initially it was really hard for Carly to meet these expectations. After all, she knew the behavior was wrong and had sought ways to avoid becoming a victim herself. Over time, however, the expected behaviors began to seem normal to Carly. They became "the way it is around here." Carly got accustomed to picking on others. Over time, she became known as a bully.

How could this be? How could Carly turn into the very thing she was afraid of?

Becoming a Member of the Herd

Humans have a desire to fit in, to be accepted in social arenas, and to feel a sense of belonging with others. Nobody likes to be left out. Finding out you were not invited to a party, being the only one not asked to the dance, or being the butt of people's jokes can lead to feelings of social exclusion. Being excluded hurts, and it's natural to look for ways to avoid further exclusions.

One way to reduce social exclusion is to adopt the behaviors of others even if they're not acceptable behaviors. Our desire and need to fit in can overpower our intentions to be good. When this happens, we adopt behaviors we would never have thought we were capable of. While we might not want to believe it, the need to belong to a group is so strong that human behavior can resemble herd behavior in animals, sometimes useful and supportive and sometimes downright violent. Somewhere in the human psyche, the need to belong is connected to the drive to survive.

An innocent factor is associated with herd behaviors in humans. People unknowingly look to see what others are doing before deciding how to behave. If a behavior appears to be socially accepted, the behavior is adopted, good or bad. People are influenced by their peers and adopt the behaviors of the "herd." This happens subconsciously in an attempt to avoid social exclusion.

Can you resist the temptation of the herd or the sorority? A classic experiment, conducted in 1971 at Stanford, sought to answer this question. The resulting report is a fascinating and chilling account of how good people who were put in evil, mob-like environments adopted behaviors that were completely in contrast to their individual personalities.

The Stanford scientists randomly assigned college men into two groups: prison guards and prisoners. The intent was to conduct a two-week investigation into the psychology of prison life; in particular, the psychological effects of being either a prisoner or a prison guard. The experiment had to be stopped after only six days because the prison guards became sadistic and the prisoners became depressed and showed signs of extreme stress.

Very quickly, the men lost sight of the fact that they were participating in an experiment and actually took on the behaviors of their assigned roles. For example, the guards, suspecting a prison break, escalated levels of abuse and voluntarily worked extra hours unpaid. And one prisoner became so depressed he cried uncontrollably and stopped eating and drinking, prompting his immediate release from the experiment.

The Stanford prison experiment showed that a situation and environment could cause negative and hostile behavior. Bad behavior is not necessarily caused solely by individual personalities. The experiment indicated that even essentially good people could behave in horrific ways when placed in an environment where horrific behaviors are accepted or expected. After the experiment, participants conveyed shock that they had behaved in ways they never thought possible.

Call it peer pressure, mob mentality, or herding behaviors: we all have the potential, even as good people, to behave in negative ways.

HOW TO DROP OUT OF THE HERD

If you've identified some of your behaviors as contributing to horizontal violence, whether you act individually or as a member of the sorority, be assured that healthier options are available. Start to de-bully your behavior with the following actions:

- REFLECT ON THE MOTIVES BEHIND YOUR BEHAVIOR
  If you can identify the reason, you can start to change your behavior. Here are some questions to ask:

  - Are you suffering from low self-esteem?

  - Do you have high self-esteem, to the extent that you see others as inferior?

  - Have you been the victim in your past and have taken on the attitude of "better a bully than a victim"?

  - Have you joined a bully sorority to avoid being a target?

  - Have you bought into the assumption that nurses need to "toughen up" to succeed in the profession?

- ASK SOMEONE FOR HELP
  This person could be someone in your organization, a colleague, a friend, or a professional counselor.

- FIND AN ACCOUNTABILITY PARTNER
  Look to this person for encouragement but also give him or her permission to give immediate feedback when your behavior is inappropriate.

DROPPING OUT TAKES MORAL COURAGE

If you are a member of a bully sorority and want to break free, you'll need to summon your moral courage. Once you recognize and make a decision to pull away from the sorority, the group may retaliate in some way. You will need to tap into your own inner strength and ask for support from others to help get you through. Here are more action steps to help you along the way:

- FIND A BUDDY

  Since many of us join the sorority and adopt herd behaviors to avoid social exclusion and pain, you are
  probably not the only one looking to get out. Observe
  some of the other nurses in your sorority for any signs
  of a partner—someone to join you as you leave the
  group. This person can help ease the pain of social exclusion and help you to foster healthier behaviors.

- APOLOGIZE

  If you've been bullying a co-worker(s), apologize for
  your behavior. An apology can be a powerful tool to
  pave the way for a healthier relationship. You may
  choose to make some changes before you apologize so
  that your words will have credibility. It's okay to seek
  help and accountability before you make yourself
  vulnerable with an apology.

- LEAVE

  Sometimes the sorority is too strong and they won't let
  you out. Also, if you are in a situation where you are
  concerned for your safety, you may make the decision
  to leave that unit, department, or even that organization and start anew.

- GET PROFESSIONAL HELP

  Whether you joined the sorority deliberately or inadvertently, your behavior has likely become a habit.
  Getting help from a professional can help you to forgive yourself and adopt strategies to prevent you from
  getting caught up in the next destructive group.

If you have recognized bully behavior in yourself, avoid
spending excess energy on guilt and self-deprecation. Nurses
who bully don't always make a conscious decision to treat their
co-workers poorly. Sometimes they adopt bully behaviors to

cope with the demands of the job, protect themselves from others (the best defense is a good offense), or because they have personal issues that infect their work environment. There is no shame in realizing you've been behaving as a bully. The shame lies when you realize it but do nothing to change.

> *People can be more forgiving than you can imagine. But you have to forgive yourself. Let go of what's bitter and move on.*
>
> ~ Bill Cosby

CHAPTER 10

IT IS TIME FOR EVERYONE TO ACT

> *A real decision is measured by the fact that you've taken a new action. If there's no action, you haven't truly decided.*
>
> ~ Tony Robbins

Bullying causes physical and emotional damage to individuals, the nursing profession, healthcare organizations, and patients. It destroys relationships, undermines efforts to improve workplace environments, results in medical errors, and sets the stage for poor patient outcomes. Bullying also prevents good people from entering and staying in the profession. Nurses have kept silent for such a long time that many think bully behavior will never go away. But there is hope.

Massive numbers of people are talking about bullying, and they want it to stop. You read about it on Twitter; it's a common topic for discussion on LinkedIn nursing groups and blogs. Nurses are talking about bullying as a tangible thing that can and should be eliminated. Like a cancerous tumor, it has to be cut out, eradicated, and destroyed. Nursing students are also very aware of the problem and consider the behavioral reputation of units as criteria for choosing their first jobs, even more than the patient population. Every generation, every position, and every organization is recognizing the problem and trying to do something about it.

As Sally Fields did in *Norma Rae*, we all need to get up on the table and shout, "We're not going to take it anymore!" Generations before us have suffered in silence while "nurses ate their young." The problem perpetuated itself because we didn't talk about it, swept it under the rug, and hoped it would just go away. However, we now see how detrimental ignoring the problem is, not only for individuals and organizations but for patients too. If we all take a stand, our collective voices can truly transform the nursing profession.

Most people in the workforce fall into one of the following categories:

- Victims of one or more bullies
- Witnesses to bullying acts
- Bullies (deliberately or accidentally)

Most of this book has outlined what to do if you are in the first category, the target of a bully. However, if we ever hope to eliminate bullying, we must make concerted efforts to address all the categories.

ACTION STEPS IF YOU ARE THE TARGET

Targets of bullies make up the largest group and need the most support. As a target, you are in the prime position to lead efforts to stop this behavior. In Chapter 7, we talked about the steps you can take if you are a victim. Write the following four words on a piece of paper and keep them with you. These represent your individual action steps:

1. Recognize
2. Separate
3. Speak up
4. Confront

Review often the steps these words represent, detailed in Chapter 7. Practice assertive communication in everyday situations. Your first attempts might feel like bumbling, but they will surprise the bully and begin to send a message. As you continue to respond assertively, the bully will find you less and less attractive as a target.

ACTION STEPS

- PURCHASE A JOURNAL
  Document events that constitute bullying behaviors that occur during your workday. Note the date, time, person, and facts.

- SHARE WITH A SAFE PERSON
  This can be someone outside the organization. Just break your silence and share your experiences and feelings.

- FIND OTHERS LIKE YOU
  If you are the target of bullying, chances are there are others. Find them. There is strength in numbers.

- REPORT TO AN AUTHORITY FIGURE
  Once you have sufficient documentation, share your journal with a trustworthy person in an authority position. If possible, begin with your manager.

- FILE A FORMAL COMPLAINT
  If your attempts to confront the bully and alert an authority figure do not result in positive change, file a formal complaint with an HR representative.

- CONSIDER THE NEED TO LEAVE
  If you've done everything you know to do and still find yourself in a toxic situation, consider changing units or organizations for your own health.

Make a habit of reminding yourself that you deserve to work in a healthy, supportive environment. You owe it to yourself to make a stand against disrespect and abuse.

STORY OF SUCCESS

Angela had been a nurse for only six months when she considered quitting. It wasn't that she didn't love her job, her patients, and some of her co-workers. Angela considered quitting because of Janice, the queen bully, and her "posse" of mini-bullies.

Every time Angela worked with the group, the torment began. Janice would change the assignments, giving Angela the most difficult patients. The group would refuse to help Janice during a crisis, openly criticize, and poke fun at her. These behaviors, of course, were hidden from the manager.

Although Angela had completed her bachelor's degree and graduated at the top of her class, she started questioning her skills, intellect, and ability to be a good nurse. She felt like a failure and dreaded coming to work.

One evening on break, Angela stopped in the library to get away from Janice and her posse. She picked up a nursing journal and read an article about horizontal violence. Angela felt as though the article were written just for her. For the first time, she saw Janice's behaviors for what they were—acts of bullying.

She recognized the problem was with Janice and not with her. Angela mentally separated herself from Janice's hostility and realized she was a target. She was relieved and asked the librarian for a copy of the article.

Angela finished the article and searched for more. To her surprise, she found numerous articles on horizontal violence and bullying in the nursing profession. Understanding the problem gave Janice validation that she was a good nurse and deserved to work in an environment that was supportive rather than toxic. After spending time researching, Angela made a plan for action.

Angela started documenting any occurrence of bullying. Once Angela had several incidents documented, she set up a meeting with her manager to share her experiences. At first, Angela was scared to meet with her manager. The night before the meeting, Angela reviewed the research again, which gave her the moral courage to speak up.

During the meeting, the manager admitted having concerns about Janice. The manager hadn't acted because she lacked concrete evidence. Nobody had ever come forward with specifics before, and Janice always behaved well when the manager was around. The manager also admitted that she was intimidated by Janice and reluctant to address her concerns, especially when nobody had formally complained.

When Angela filed a complaint against Janice, her manager vowed to hold Janice accountable for her behavior. The manager also confronted Janice and the others, telling each one individually she was on disciplinary action and could eventually be terminated if the behavior didn't change.

Once Angela had support from her manager, she started confronting Janice during her bullying attacks. For example, when Janice yelled at her in the nurses' station in front of others, Angela replied assertively, "Excuse me, Janice. It's inappropriate to yell in an area where patients and their families can hear. If you would like to discuss this in private as professionals, we can go to the break room." Then Angela turned her back and walked away.

The first time Angela responded in this way, Janice just stood with her mouth open, caught off guard. As Angela found ways to confront Janice regarding each of her bully behaviors, Janice decreased and eventually stopped the behavior. Janice's posse also stopped their bad behavior toward Angela.

As the bully behavior subsided, Angela's confidence grew and she started looking forward to coming to work again. She knew she was a good nurse and developed good relationships with her patients and co-workers.

Like Angela, you can take steps to minimize the bully's effect on you. By changing your response, you can reduce or stop the bad behavior. If you feel uncomfortable going through these steps, talk to someone who can support and encourage you, even if that person is outside the organization. Take baby steps. And by all means, tap into your moral courage and remember that you deserve to work in a supportive environment!

> *I learned that courage was not the absence of fear, but the triumph over it. The brave man is not he who does not feel afraid, but he who conquers that fear.*
> ~ Nelson Mandela

ACTION STEPS IF YOU ARE WITNESS TO ACTS OF BULLYING

Many of us have witnessed bullying acts against others and have kept silent. Sometimes, we are just thankful the bully's focus is on somebody else and not us! Other times, we are caught off guard or simply don't know what to say or do. By our silence, we unwittingly condone and contribute to a culture of bullying.

It's time we start raising our collective voices to stop the cycle of bullying, one incident at a time. Make the decision now that when you witness acts of bullying, you will take action.

Remember to tap into moral courage, for defending somebody else may be the hardest, most uncomfortable selfless act you take. But you can do it. Commit the following four words to memory. These represent your action steps as a witness.

1. Recognize
2. Document
3. Confront
4. Support

Review often the steps these words represent, detailed in Chapter 8. Make documentation a habit. Practice assertive communication in everyday situations. Then you'll be ready when it's time to stand up. Your first attempts won't be perfect, and you might be scared to death, but you will build strength and skill with each attempt.

ACTION STEPS

- DECIDE TO MAKE A POSITIVE DIFFERENCE
  Make the decision up front to confront any acts of bullying behavior immediately when you see them happening.

- GATHER LIKE-MINDED CO-WORKERS
  Find others who are just as fed up with the bad behaviors and are willing to confront and support.

- SPEAK UP
  When you see an act of bullying, use assertive communication to name the behavior.

- RECORD WHAT YOU WITNESS
  Document any acts of bullying you witness with date, time, person, and facts.

- REPORT TO AN AUTHORITY FIGURE
  Once you have sufficient documentation, share the information with a trustworthy person in an authority position. If possible, begin with your manager.

- CONSIDER FILING A FORMAL COMPLAINT
  If your attempts to confront the bully and alert an authority figure do not result in positive change, consider filing a formal complaint with an HR representative. While a formal complaint is an extreme step, the culture of your unit is at stake. If a bully culture isn't impacting you today, it may do so tomorrow.

- SUPPORT THE VICTIM
  Let the victim know bully behavior is always inappropriate. Offer encouragement.

STORY OF SUCCESS

Beth was a SuperNurse. She took great pride in knowing she intimidated both new and experienced nurses. Beth was frequently overheard yelling and criticizing nurses, nursing assistants, and therapists. Even physicians weren't safe from her tirades.

Beth was always in charge and could make life a living hell for people who crossed her. Nobody ever confronted Beth for fear of retaliation. Beth bullied others into a zone of silent acceptance of "this is the way it is around here."

Doris and Vicki were nurses who worked on the same unit as Beth. They began discussing the issue of horizontal violence after attending a workshop by an outside consultant. The consultant's descriptions of bullying behavior really hit home with Doris and Vicki as they each recognized Beth's behavior as bullying. During the workshop, they made a pact to address Beth's overt bullying by naming the behavior. Although they were worried about how Beth would react, Doris and Vicki thought they could take this step.

One week later, Doris overheard Beth ranting and raving at a new nurse in the hallway. Her typical reaction had been to walk away. But then Doris remembered the pact. Doris took a deep breath, walked towards Beth and said, "Beth, I can hear you screaming and yelling all the way down the hallway. I'm sure patients and their families can hear you too. Please address whatever problem you see in a more respectful manner."

Beth just stood with her mouth open, dumbfounded. She looked at Doris and walked away without saying a word. Doris maintained eye contact with Beth until she left and then provided support to the new nurse who had been Beth's target.

As Doris and Vicky continued to name Beth's bullying behaviors, the culture of the unit began to change. Other nurses began to name the behavior in response to Beth's yelling and screaming. Over time, Beth's yelling incidents decreased dramatically.

One person who stands up to the bully can inspire others to do the same. The world will not end if you stand up to a bully. In fact, others around you will see that an assertive response is possible. A mirror phenomenon can occur where others start to model or "mirror" your assertive behaviors. Not only will you be providing a role model for professional behavior, but you will be sending a message to others that bullying doesn't have to be tolerated.

Action Steps if You Are the Bully

Somebody is the bully. After all, nurses can't "eat their young" without an "eater." You may have recognized yourself as either leading bullying efforts or having become an accidental bully. In either case, you need to stop your destructive behavior immediately. The steps to guide you through the process are presented in detail in Chapter 9. Begin by recognizing and accepting that you are behaving as a bully.

Admitting that you are acting as a bully can be a shock to your self-esteem. Uncovering as much as you can about your reasons for bullying can help you see yourself as a good person who has gone down the wrong path.

Changing your behavior and habitual responses, especially under stress, will be difficult, and it won't happen instantly. However, you can make real changes. Confide in someone you trust and ask that person to support you along the way. Seek professional counseling, if needed, to help you during the transition.

> *All the beautiful sentiments in the world weigh less than a single lovely action.*
>
> ~ James Russell Lowell

STORY OF SUCCESS

After attending a workshop on social media, Cindy was excited to set up her profile page on LinkedIn. Cindy was passionate about critical care nursing and looked forward to networking with other "smart" nurses like her. Cindy was proud of her clinical skills and frequently shared her expertise with others.

What Cindy didn't know was that while her clinical skills were excellent, she was known as a bully among the nurses throughout the hospital where she worked. Medical surgical nurses despised giving Cindy report if they had to transfer a patient to her; new nurses were petrified if they were put with Cindy for the day; and even physicians avoided her. Cindy was aware that others were intimidated when around her, but she thought this was because she was so smart. "After all," reasoned Cindy, "this is critical care! These patients are sick and need someone like me to teach everyone else what to do."

One evening at home, Cindy logged onto LinkedIn and read a discussion about horizontal violence. While reading the stories shared by other nurses who were struggling with a bully, Cindy saw herself. For the first time, Cindy saw her behavior through the eyes of her co-workers and was ashamed. What she thought was being smart was, in reality, being a bully.

Days went by with Cindy feeling terrible about her behavior. Then, Cindy went back online and searched for more information regarding horizontal violence. When she had a few days off, Cindy made a list of everyone she remembered being mean to. Over the course of the next few weeks, Cindy personally apologized to each one and asked that they call her on her behavior if she treated them poorly again. Over time, Cindy learned to forgive herself and to find new ways of coping with the stress of being a nurse.

Like Cindy, if you recognize yourself in the descriptions of a bully, please forgive yourself and get help. We are all human beings and make mistakes. The key is to take responsibility for our mistakes and learn from them.

MORAL COURAGE IS YOUR RESERVOIR OF STRENGTH

Whether you are a victim, a witness, or a bully committed to positive change, moments will come when the burden of bullying and your efforts to stop it will feel too heavy. There will be moments when you know you should intervene during a bullying act, but the fear in your throat tells you to look the other way. There will be moments when you know that pulling away is the right thing to do even while you recognize that going against the sorority might turn you into a target.

We all face such moments—ones in which we have tough decisions to make. The decisions we know to be right can make us feel incredibly uncomfortable. In these moments, we need to rely on our deep-seated moral courage. Moral courage can act as our reservoir of strength, enabling us to push through our discomfort with confrontation, defending others, leaving the sorority, or leaving the organization.

Once you make a decision to act, take a deep breath and visualize dipping deep into your reservoir of moral courage. Then move forward. Be a hero. Wear the badge. Stop the bullying. Just remember, you and your colleagues deserve to work in an environment that is nurturing, supportive, and professional.

> *We can do no great things—only small things with great love.*
>
>   ~ Mother Theresa

BONUS SECTION FOR ORGANIZATIONS

> *Lack of knowledge of, or unwillingness to recognize, or outright denial of the existence of the serial bully is the most common reason for an unsatisfactory outcome of a bullying case for both the employee and employer.*
> ~ Tim Field

In Chapter 1, we discussed the mandate by the Joint Commission for all organizations to institute codes of conduct or a zero tolerance policy for bullying. However, there is a difference between having a code of conduct and embedding the code into the culture of an organization. Some organizations spend an incredible amount of time and energy developing their code of conduct, getting all employees to sign the code as an indication they will abide by it, only for the documents to get shoved deep into the recesses of a file cabinet, never to be seen again.

Codes of conduct need to be infused into everyday operations in all departments. Expectations for conduct need to be objective and measurable, not only for every employee but for every person who walks into the organization. To be effective, codes of conduct can't consist of promises on paper but must be standards of behavior infused and enforced in every aspect of the organization.

When her organization announced that it was going to address horizontal violence, Sarah was relieved because, as a new nurse in the Emergency Room, she was a victim. Two bullies constantly picked on her, made fun of her, and dumped on her. The organization established a code of conduct which addressed horizontal violence with the nursing staff. In-services were mandated on the topic, bulletin boards were posted, and e-mails were sent. Every nurse in the organization heard the term "horizontal violence."

Sarah looked forward to a more supportive work environment once every employee signed the code of conduct forms. However, on her shift following the signing, the two bullies were at it again. Not only did they continue picking on Sarah, but the code of conduct seemed to act as a catalyst for their bullying behaviors.

The bullies ganged up on Sarah and then sarcastically criticized each other saying, "Uh oh. I think that was an example of horizontal violence," winking at each other. "I'm going to tell on you," they laughed, enjoying their own joke.

By itself, having a code of conduct doesn't solve the problem. Organization leaders who think it does are mistaken. A code of conduct is a good first step but only if individuals are empowered and motivated to enforce it.

> *Policies don't solve problems. People do.*
> ~ Renee Thompson

EDUCATE AND EMPOWER UNIT MANAGERS

Organizations that empower their managers to address bad behavior are organizations that successfully create healthy work environments. Steps to empower managers include educating managers and then supporting their disciplinary actions.

There is an assumption that once a person gets to a management position, that person has the skills to deal with employee issues. The assumption is false. The skills to address behavior and performance do not magically appear with the title of manager. These skills, however, can be learned. Organizations that provide education to managers, along with ongoing in-services, seminars, and workshops to address common problems, not only improve the skill levels of managers but also improve management satisfaction.

Managers who leave their positions often do so because they are overwhelmed with poor employee behavior and don't feel competent or empowered to address it. Once managers receive education and develop the skill set to address bad behavior, organizations need to support their efforts to proceed with disciplinary action, even if that means terminating an employee during a nursing shortage.

Walking an employee down the disciplinary action path takes time, energy, and courage. Typically the path starts with verbal warnings, proceeds to written warnings, followed by suspension, and ultimately termination if the behavior doesn't improve. In some situations, immediate termination is indicated: violation of patient safety standards, abandoning patients, violence of any type, etc. However, sometimes the manager believes it is appropriate to terminate an employee but needs approval from the organization, typically an HR professional.

Earlier, we looked at the incident in which Judy, the unit manager, used disciplinary action in the case of Sylvia and Martha, two nurses who were disrupting the unit with bullying and poor patient care. Initially, when Judy tried to put Sylvia and Martha on the disciplinary path, the HR representative pushed back. Judy either needed one more signature, another witness, a stronger reason, etc. Even when Sylvia walked off the unit, which is a huge patient safety issue, Judy was initially told she couldn't do more than give Sylvia a written warning for this behavior. Instead of giving up, Judy scheduled time to meet with the HR leaders, presented her unit's "expectations for behavior" plan, and worked with HR to support her accountability plan. Collaboratively, Judy was able to follow through on disciplining Sylvia and Martha according to the plan.

As a manager whose disciplinary procedures were initially unsupported by the organization, Judy showed remarkable persistence. It's unrealistic for an organization to expect all managers to pursue disciplinary action without support. When a unit manager knows his or her decisions about bad behavior and poor performance will be supported, the manager becomes empowered and motivated to do his or her job effectively. In addition, managerial support, or lack thereof, is an element of organizational culture that influences everyone's behavior.

Combating horizontal violence takes a village. An organization must go beyond having a piece of paper regarding conduct. It must educate and support managers every step of the way.

About the Author

Renee Thompson DNP, RN, CMSRN has been a human for 40+ years and a nurse for more than 20. Several years ago she took a leap of faith and started her own business, RTConnections. As a speaker, consultant, and coach, she is trying to make a difference in the lives of nurses and the patients they serve. Renee is well known for her energizing and entertaining speaking style, along with her ability to simplify complex concepts in a way that helps nurses succeed.

Renee speaks nationwide to healthcare organizations and academic institutions, motivating audiences through keynote addresses, professional conferences, workshops, and seminars. Renee inspires nurses and other healthcare professionals in a fun and interactive fashion, sharing her vision through storytelling with meaningful life lessons and examples. Her presentations focus on improving clinical and professional competence; addressing nurse-to-nurse bullying; effective communication and leadership; embracing social media in nursing; building a positive and healthy workplace; and nurturing a culture of respect.

Renee believes that patients deserve to be cared for by competent, compassionate nurses and that nurses deserve to believe they make a difference.

Renee lives in Pittsburgh, Pennsylvania with her husband Ashley, her daughter Courtney, and Courtney's three cats, Oreo, Nikoli, and Dakota.

Renee offers keynote presentations, workshops, and seminars to organizations. To learn more or to schedule Renee for your next nursing event, contact Renee through her website: www.rtconnections.com.

CONNECT WITH RENEE

Website ...... : www.rtconnections.com
LinkedIn ..... : Linkedin.com/in/rtconnections
Facebook .... : http://RTConnect.fbfollow.me
Twitter....... : twitter.com/rtconnections
Blog .... : blog.rtconnections.com

WHY CHOOSE RENEE FOR YOUR NEXT EVENT?

Founder of RTConnections, Renee Thompson DNP, RN, CMSRN is a sought-after speaker, consultant, and coach. Healthcare, academic, and professional nursing organizations love to book Renee for the following reasons:

EXPERIENCE
Renee has given hundreds of lectures, workshops, and seminars to hospitals, schools of nursing, associations, and businesses.

FASCINATING FACTS
By keeping up to date on the most current nursing trends, Renee provides audiences with the latest information needed for success.

FUN AND HUMOROUS
Renee is well known for her energetic and entertaining speaking style, sharing humorous stories from the front lines of nursing. Renee is spontaneous and interacts with audiences to keep everyone engaged.

REAL AND AUTHENTIC
Renee has an amazing ability to connect with her audiences as she shares stories from her own journey to competent, professional practice.

In addition to addressing the topic of nurse-to-nurse bullying, Renee guides audiences to improve clinical and professional competence, effectively communicate and lead, embrace social media in nursing, build a positive and healthy workplace, and nurture a culture of respect.

> *To book Renee Thompson for your next event, go to www.rtconnections.com.*

SUGGESTED READINGS

Aleccia, J. (2008). Hospital bullies take a toll on patient safety. http://www.msnbc.msn.com/id/25594124/ns/health-health_care/t/hospital-bullies-take-toll-patient-safety/#.

American Nurses Association (2001). *Code for ethics for nurses with interpretative statements.* Silver Springs, MD: American Nurses Publishing.

Andersson, L.M., Pearson, C.M. (1999). Tit for tat? The spiraling effect of incivility in the workplace. *Academy of Management Review,* 24, 452-457.

Baldoni, J. (June 13, 2011). You've discovered wrongdoing. Now what? Message posted to http://www.cbsnews.com/8301-505125_162-49440217/youve-discovered-wrong-doing-now-what/?tag=bnetdomain.

Bartholomew, K. (2011). Lateral violence in nursing: breaking the spell. *Nurse Together.* Retrieved on August 10, 2011, from www.nursetogether.com.

Brinkman, R., Kirschner, R. (2002). *Dealing with people you can't stand.* New York: McGraw Hill.

Brown, L., Middaugh, D. (2009). Nursing hazing: a costly reality. *Medsurg Nursing,* 28(5), 305–307.

Christmas, K. (2007). Workplace abuse: finding solutions. *Nursing Economics,* 25(6), 365-367.

Clark, C.M. (2008). Student voices on faculty incivility in nursing education: a conceptual model. *Nursing Education Perspectives*, 29(5), 284–289.

Clark. C. (2008). The dance of incivility in nursing education as described by nursing faculty and students. *Advances in Nursing Science*, 31(4), 37–54.

Dellasega, C. (2005). *Mean girls grown up: adult women who are still queen bees, middle bees, and afraid-to-bees.* Hoboken, New Jersey: John Wiley and Sons.

Dellasega, C.A. (2009). Bullying among nurses. *American Journal of Nursing*, 109(1), 52-58.

Dumont, C., Riggleman, K., Meisinger, S., Lein, A. (2011). Horizontal violence survey. *Nursing2011*, 4, 9–10.

Felbinger, D. M. (2008). Incivility and bullying in the workplace and nurses' shame responses. *Journal of Obstetric, Gynecologic, & Neonatal Nursing*, 37, 234-242.

Felbinger, D. M. (2009). Bullying, incivility, and disruptive behaviors in the healthcare setting: identification, impact, and intervention. *Frontiers of Health Services Management*, 36, 13-23.

Freire, P., Ramos, M.B., Macedo, D. (2000). *Pedagogy of the oppressed.* New York: Continuum Publishing Company.

Gallagher, A. (March 21, 2010). Moral distress and moral courage in everyday nursing practice. *The Online Journal of Issues in Nursing, 16* (2).

Griffin, M. (2004). Teaching cognitive rehearsal as a shield for lateral violence: an intervention for newly licensed nurses. *Journal for Continuing Education of Nurses*, 35(6), 257-263.

Griffin, C. (2011). Healthy work environments: empowerment strategies for medical-surgical nurses dealing with lateral violence. *MedSurg Matters*, 20(5), 4-5.

Guglielmi, C. L. (2010). Embracing the freedom to eliminate disruptive behavior. *AORN Journal*, 92(4), 375-377.

Horn, S. (1996). *Tongue Fu! How to deflect, disarm, and defuse any verbal conflict.* New York: St. Martin's Press.

Hutton, S.A. (2006). Workplace incivility: state of the science. *The Journal of Nursing Administration*, 36, 22-27.

Johnson, S.L., Rea, R.E. (2009). Workplace bullying: concerns for nurse leaders. *Journal for Nursing Administration*, 39(2), 84–90.

Johnson, S.L. (2009). International perspectives on workplace bullying among nurses: a review. *International Nursing Review*, 56(1), 34-40.

Johnston, M., Phanhtharath, P., Jackson, B.S. (2009). The bullying aspect of workplace violence in nursing. *Critical Care Nursing Quarterly*, 32(4), 36-42.

Jones, C.B., Gates, M. (2007). The costs and benefits of nurse turnover: a business case for nurse retention. *The Online Journal of Issues in Nursing*, 12(3).

Kelly, D. (2006). Workplace bullying, women, and workchoices. Retrieved on August 10, 2011, from http://ro.uow.edu.au/cgi/viewcontent.cgi?article.

Kupperschmidt, B., Kientz, E., Ward, J. Reinholz, B. (2010). A healthy work environment. It begins with you. *The Online Journal of Nursing Issues in Nursing*, 15(1), 1-10.

Lachman, V.D. (2007). Moral courage in action: case studies. *Medsurg Nursing*, 16(4), 275-277.

Leiper, J. (2005). Nurse against nurse: how to stop horizontal violence. *Nursing2005*, 35(3), 44-45.

Lewis, M.A. (2006). Nurse bullying: organizational considerations in the maintenance and perpetration of healthcare bullying cultures. *Journal of Nursing Management*, 14, 52-58.

Longo, J., Sherman, R.O. (2007). Leveling horizontal violence. *Nursing Management*, 38(3). 34-47, 50-51.

Lutgen-Sandvik, P., Tracy, S.J., Alberts, J.K. (2007). Burned by bullying in the American workplace: prevalence, perception, degree, and impact. *Journal of Management Studies*, 44, 837-862.

McKenna, B.G, et al. (2003). Horizontal violence: experiences of registered nurses in their first year of practice. *Journal of Advanced Nursing*, 42(1), 90-96.

Murray, J.S. (2007). Before blowing the whistle, learn to protect yourself. *American Nurse Today*, 2(3), 40-42.

Murray, J.S. (2009). Workplace bullying in nursing: a problem that can't be ignored. *Medsurg Nursing Journal*, 18(5), 273-276.

Myer, J.R. (2006). Elements of behavior. *General Entomology ENT 425.* Retrieved on August 10, 2011 from http://www.cals.ncsu.edu/course/ent425/tutorial/Behavior/index.html.

Patterson, K., Grenny, J., McMillan, R., Switzler, A. (2002). *Crucial conversations: tools for talking when stake are high.* New York:McGraw-Hill.

Quine, L. (2001). Workplace bullying in nurses. *Journal of Health Psychology,* 6(1), 73-84.

Ramos, M.C. (2006). Eliminate destructive behaviors through example and evidence. *Nursing Management,* 37(9), 34-41.

Randle, J. (2003). Bullying in the nursing profession. *Journal of Advanced Nursing,* 43(4), 395-401.

Rowell, P.A. (2005). Being a 'target' at work or William Tell asks how the apple felt. *Journal of Nursing Administration,* 35(9), 377-379.

Sheridan-Leos, N. (2008). Understanding lateral violence in nursing. *Clinical Journal of Oncology Nursing,* 12(3), 399-403.

Sincox, A.K., Fitzpatrick, M. (2009). Lateral violence: calling out the elephant in the room. Retrieved June 13, 2011 from http://nursingnovellas.com.

Sofield, L., Salmond, S.W. (2003). Workplace violence: a focus on verbal abuse and intent to leave the organization. *Orthopaedic Nursing,* 22, 274-283.

Stanley, K.M., Martin, M.M., Michel, Y., Welton, J.M. (2007). Examining lateral violence in the nursing workforce. *Issues in Mental Health Nursing*, 28, 1247–1265.

Stokowski, L.A. (2011, March 24). The downward spiral: incivility in nursing. *Medscape*. Retrieved on August 10, 2011, from http://www.medscape.com/viewarticle/739328.

Stokowski, L.A. (2010, September 30). A matter of respect and dignity: bullying in the nursing profession. *Medscape*. Retrieved on August 10, 2011, from http://www.medscape.com/viewarticle/729474.

Taylor, B. (2001). Identifying and transforming dysfunctional nurse-nurse relationships through reflective practice and action research. *International Journal of Nursing Practice*, 7, 406–413.

The Joint Commission. (2008). Behaviors that undermine a culture of safety. *Sentinel Event Alert*, 40, 1-3.

Thomas, S.P. (2003). Horizontal hostility: nurses against themselves: how to resolve this threat to retention. *American Journal of Nursing*, 103(10), 87-88.

Vessey, J.A., Demarco, R.F., Gaffney, D.A., Budin, W.C. (2009). Bullying of staff registered nurses in the workplace: a preliminary study for developing personal and organizational strategies for the transformation of hostile to healthy workplace environments. *Journal of Professional Nursing*, 25(5), 299-306.

Wachs, J. (2009). Workplace incivility, bullying, and mobbing. *Journal of American Association of Occupational Health Nurses*, 57(2), 88.

Watson, S., Hinton, A. (September 11, 2010). Observations of behavior on the grey wolf. Message posted to http://swtdesigns.blogspot.com/2010/09/observations-of-behavior-on-grey-wolf.html.

World, H. (2008). Lateral violence can end nursing careers. *Management & Leadership Specialty Guide.* Retrieved on September 5, 2011 from http://news.nurse.com/apps/pbcs.dll/article?AID=2007701100 50.

CONTACT HOURS

CONTACT HOUR APPROVAL

"Do No Harm" Applies to Nurses Too, has been approved for two (2) contact hours by the Florida Board of Nursing (provider #50-14843), the California Board of Nursing (provider #16133), and Robert Morris University, a regionally accredited institution of higher education (ANCC approved).

INSTRUCTIONS

1. Complete the demographic data section on the next page. Your license number is required if you wish to be eligible for either Florida or California contact hours. Otherwise, we DO NOT need your RN license number.

2. Complete the test questions on page 169.

3. Complete the evaluation on page 171.

4. Photocopy the demographic, questions, and evaluation pages. Mail copies along with a check for $10 made payable to RTConnections to:

> RTConnections
> 146 Aidan Ct
> Pittsburgh, PA 15226

A certificate of two (2) contact hours will be mailed to you at the address indicated in the demographic section.

"Do No Harm" Applies to Nurses Too
CONTACT HOURS DEMOGRAPHICS

Please Print

Name _____

Address 1 _____

Address 2 _____

City _____

State _____ Zip Code _____

Email _____

RN License # _____

RN Licenses # required for California or Florida only

I, _____
Signature

affirm that I read the book, "Do No Harm" Applies to Nurses Too! shown here for contact hours.

"Do No Harm" Applies to Nurses Too

CONTACT HOURS QUESTIONS

Please read the following questions and circle the best response:

1. Which of the following behaviors are considered attractive to a bully?
    a. Displaying diminished self-confidence
    b. Demonstrating passive behavior
    c. Walking a different path
    d. All of the above

2. Which of the following communication style can be described as involving force, manipulation, and coercion?
    a. Aggressive
    b. Passive
    c. Passive-aggressive
    d. Assertive

3. One theory behind nurse-to-nurse bullying is that nursing taps into female-female aggression.
    a. True
    b. False

4. All bullies have issues with low self-esteem.
    a. True
    b. False

5. Which of the following strategies are recommended for individuals who become targets of bullying?
    a. Keep silent
    b. Name the behavior
    c. Avoid confronting the bully
    d. Retaliate against the bully

"Do No Harm" Applies to Nurses Too

CONTACT HOURS EVALUATION

1 = Poor

2 = Fair

3 = Good

4 = Very Good

5 = Excellent

Using the scale above, please rate the following:

Degree that you were able to recognize bullying
behavior. _____

Degree that you were able to develop strategies
to address bullying behavior _____

Comments:

Made in the USA
Lexington, KY
16 October 2018